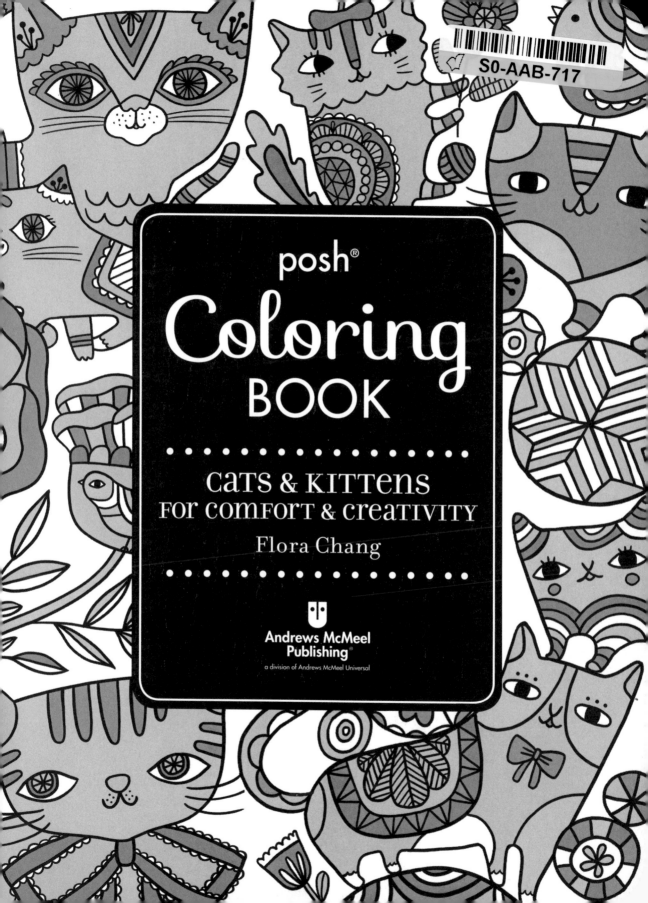

posh®

Coloring
BOOK

· · · · · · · · · · · · · · ·

CATS & KITTENS
FOR COMFORT & CREATIVITY

Flora Chang

· · · · · · · · · · · · · · ·

Andrews McMeel
Publishing®

a division of Andrews McMeel Universal

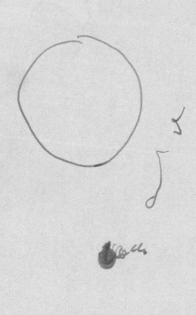

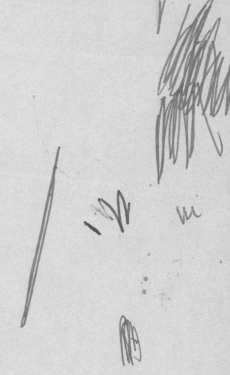

POSH® COLORING BOOK
CATS & KITTENS FOR COMFORT & CREATIVITY

Andrews McMeel Publishing
a division of Andrews McMeel Universal
1130 Walnut Street, Kansas City, Missouri 64106

www.andrewsmcmeel.com

16 17 18 19 20 MLY 10 9 8 7 6 5 4 3 2 1

ISBN: 978-1-4494-7873-5

ATTENTION: SCHOOLS AND BUSINESSES
Andrews McMeel books are available at quantity discounts
with bulk purchase for educational, business, or sales
promotional use. For information, please e-mail the
Andrews McMeel Publishing Special Sales Department:
specialsales@amuniversal.com.

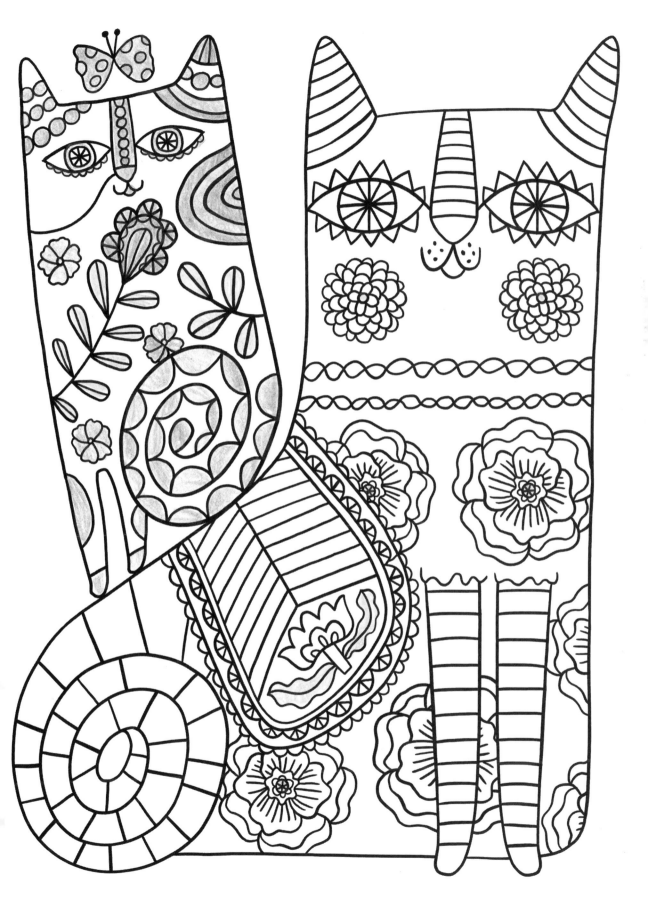

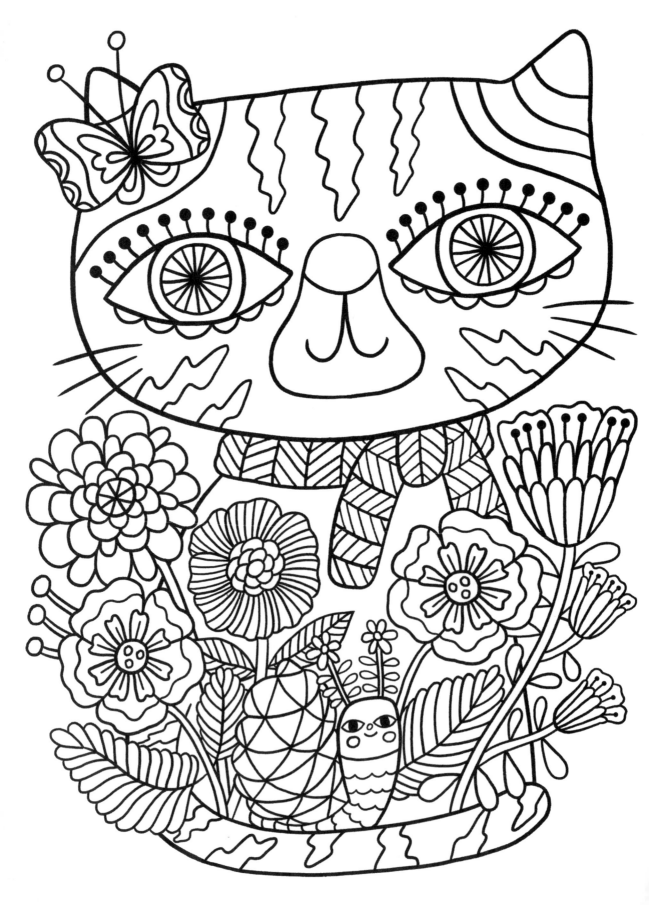

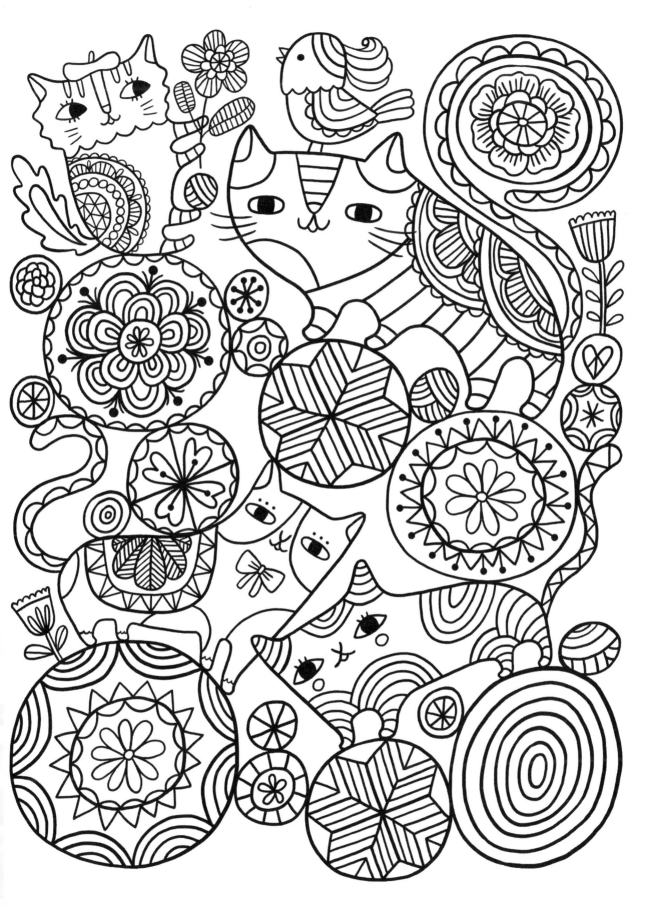

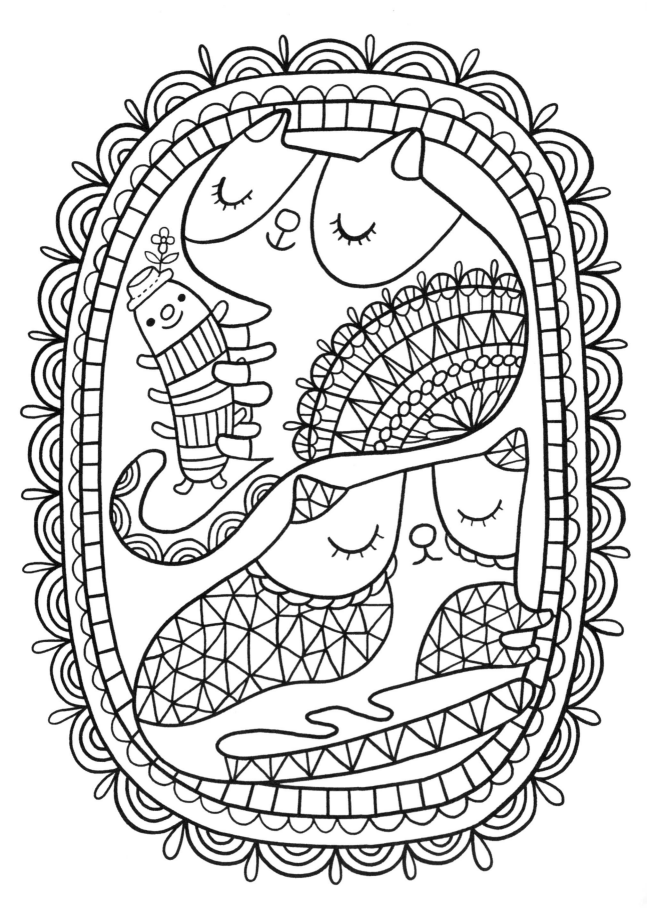

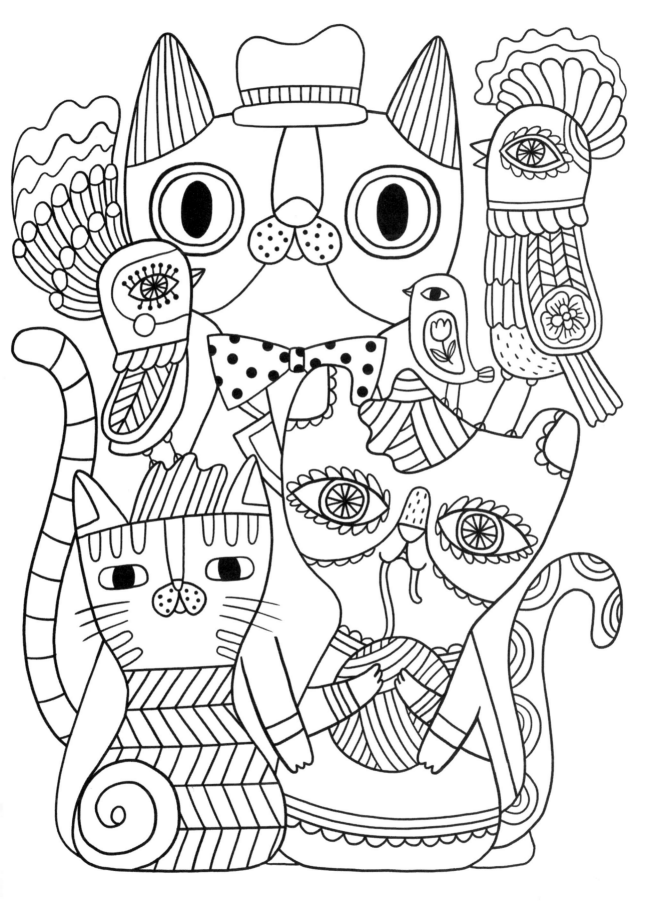

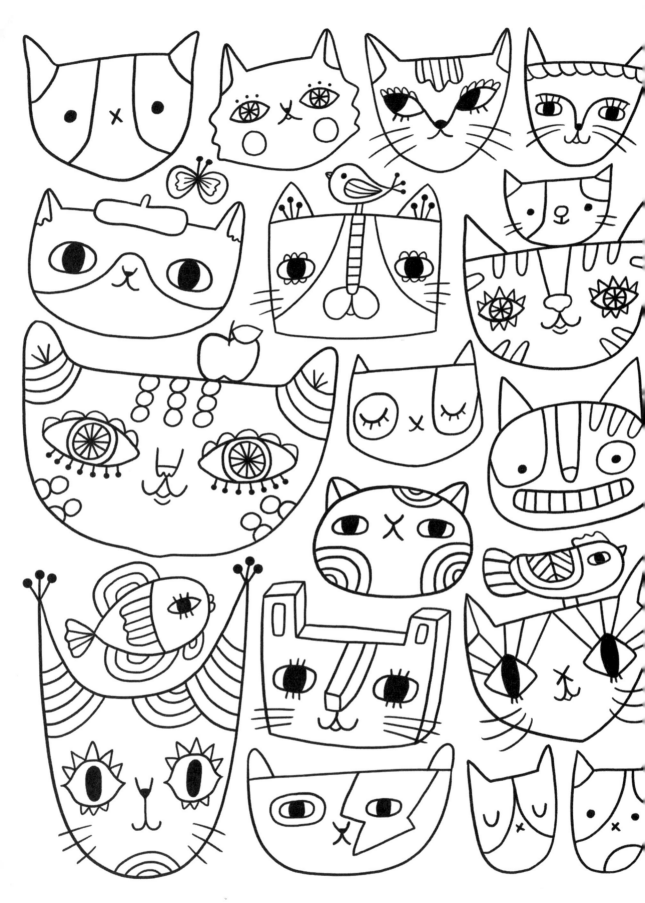

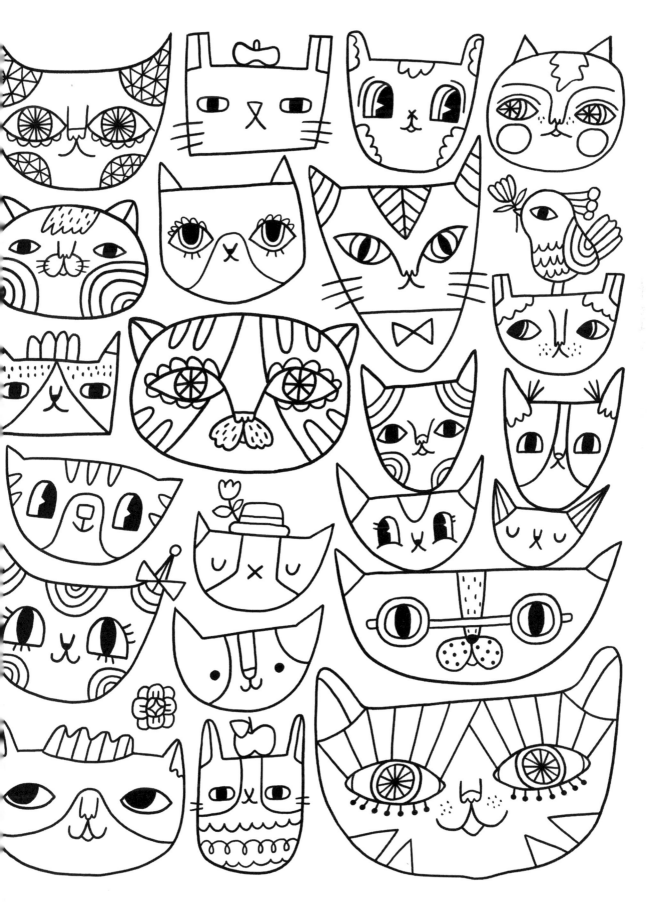

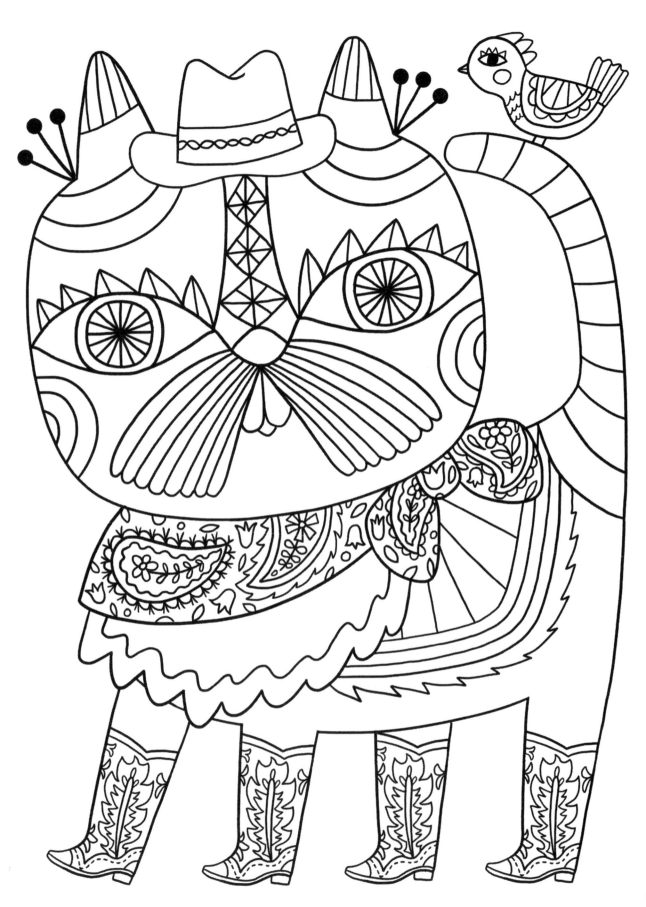

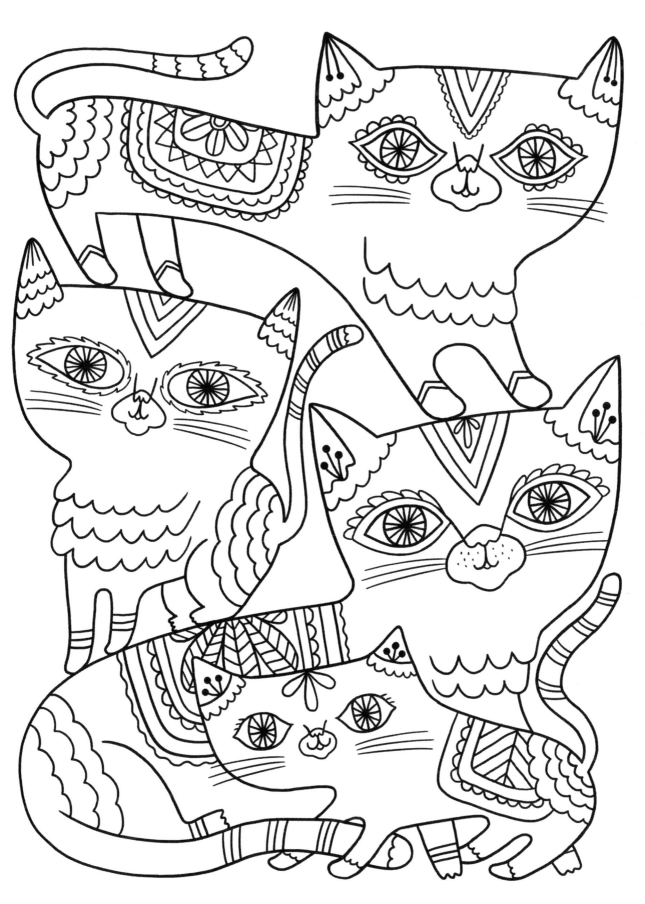

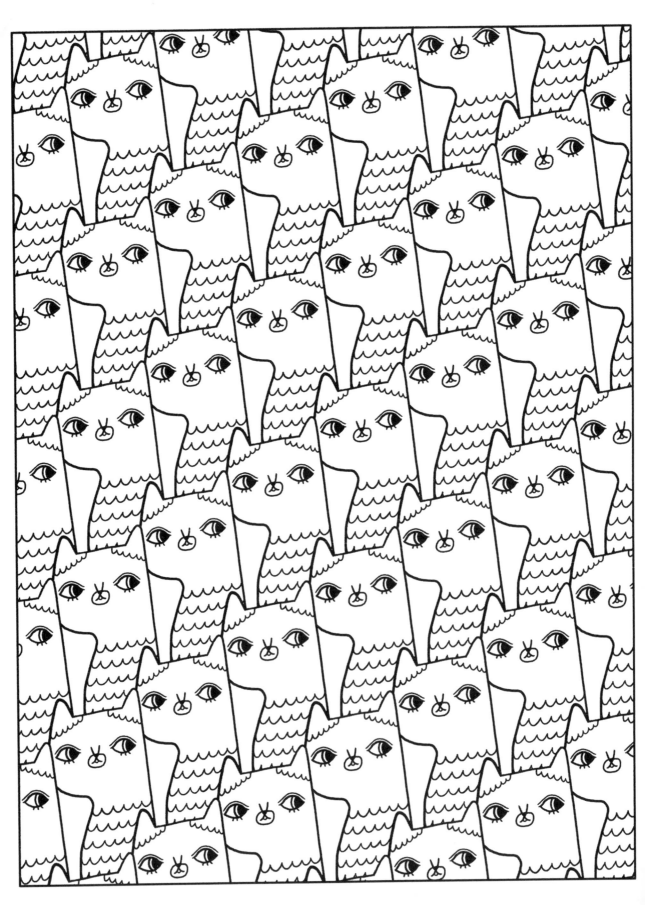

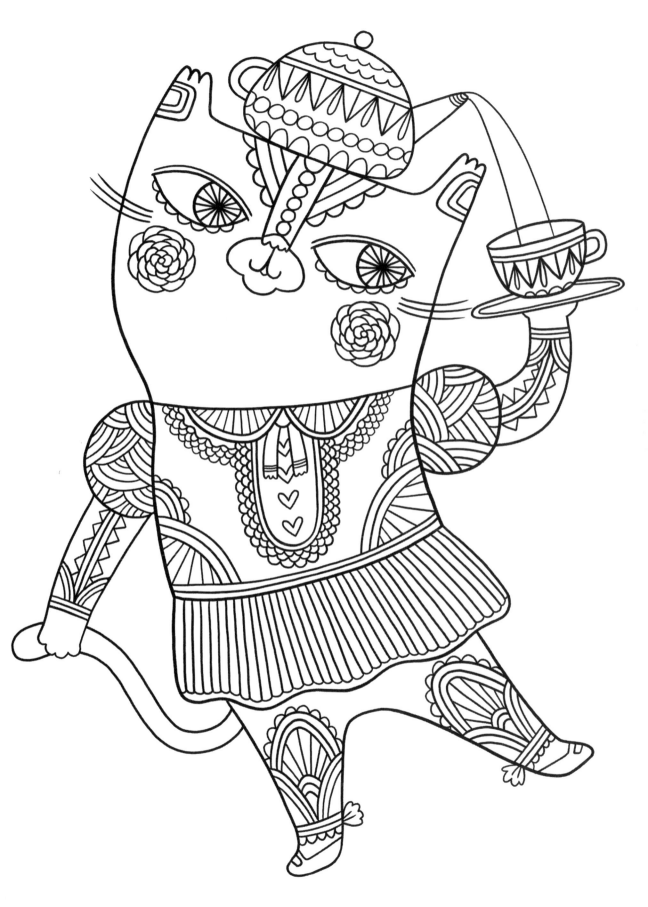

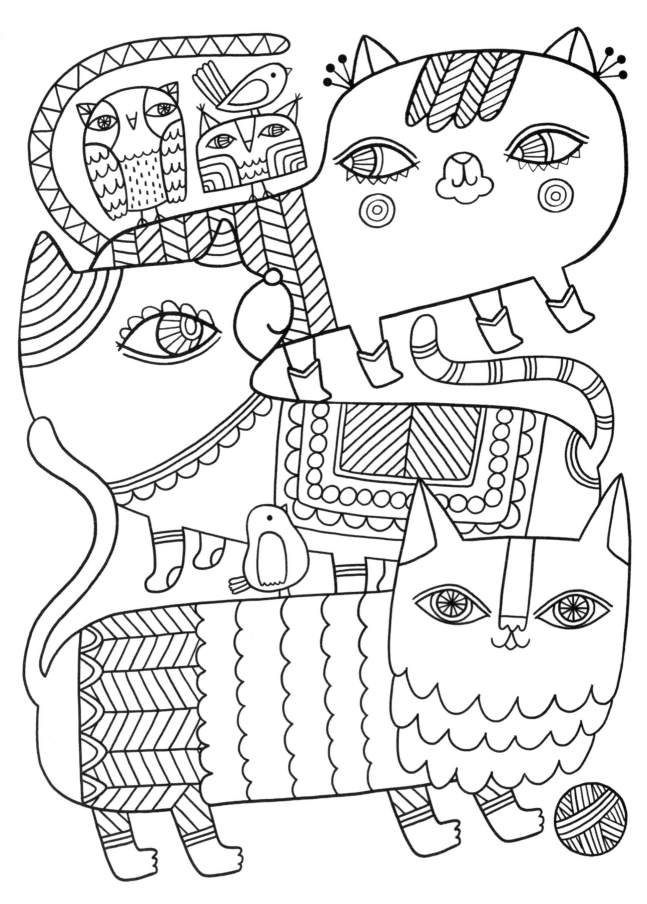

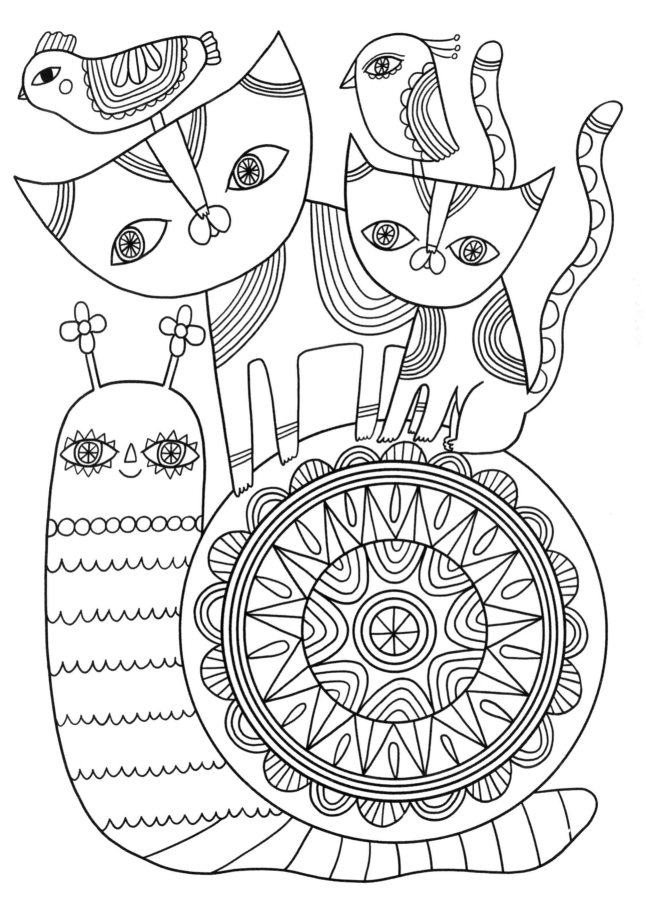

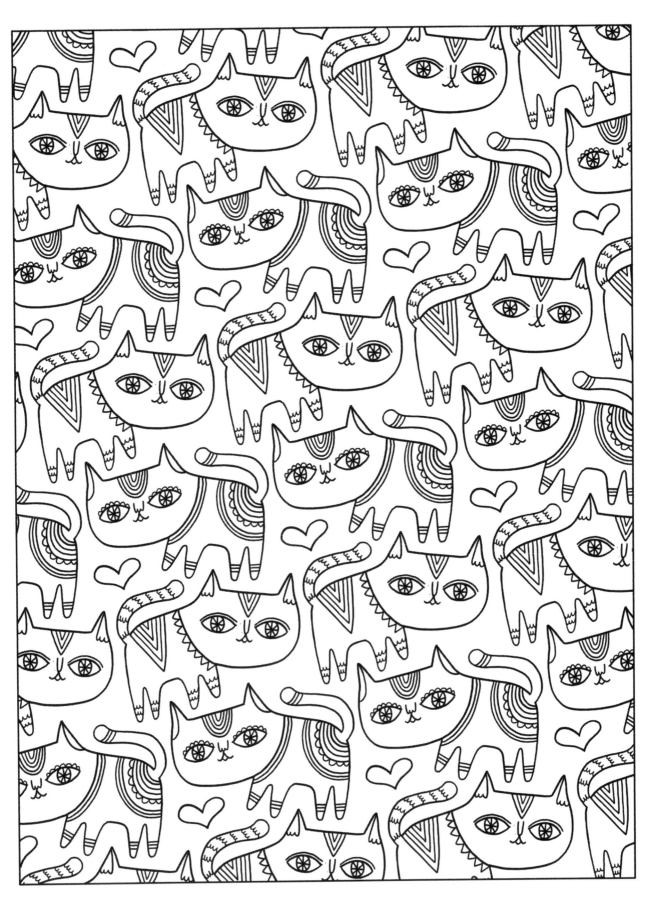

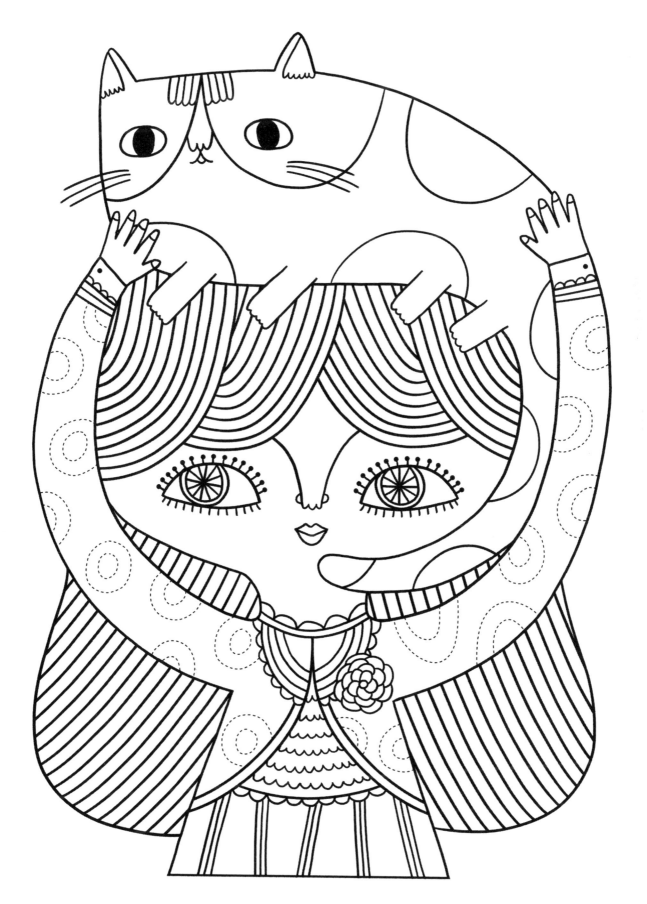

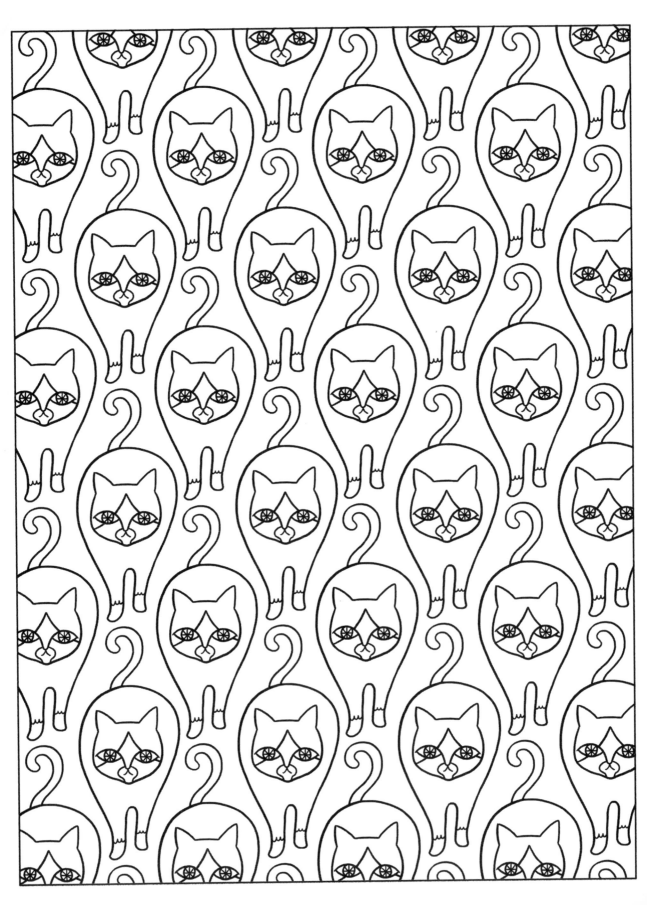

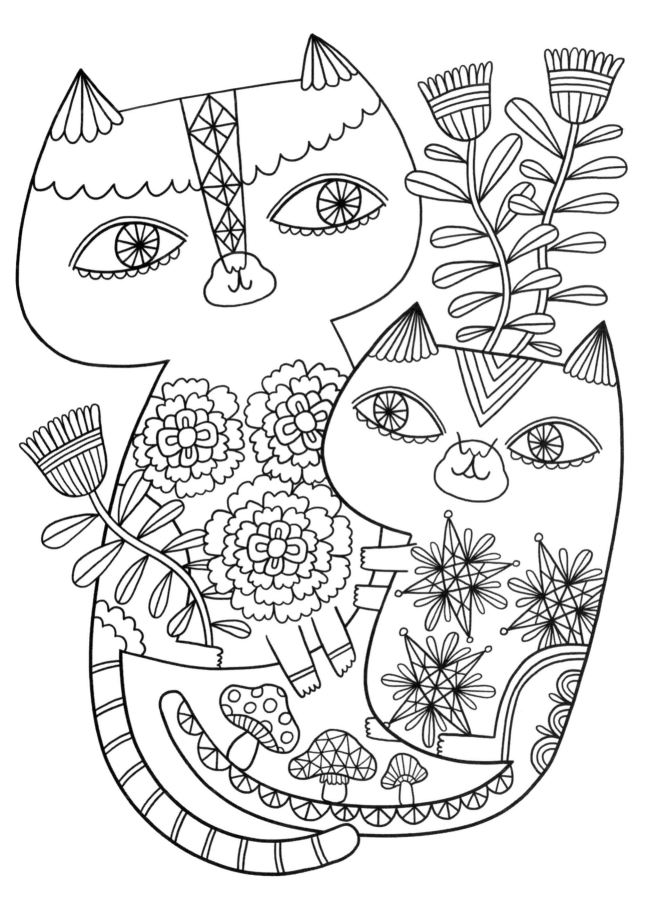

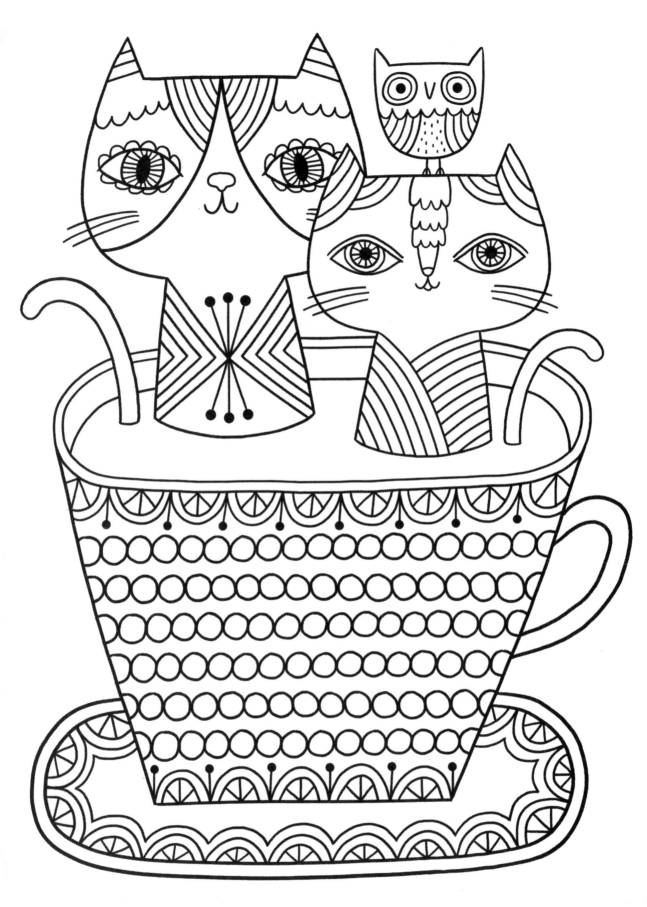

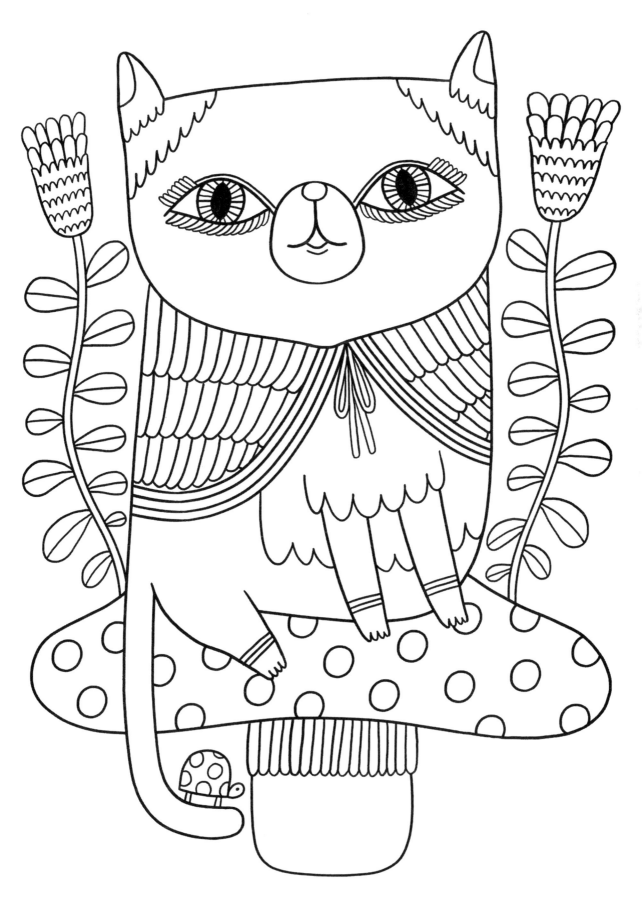

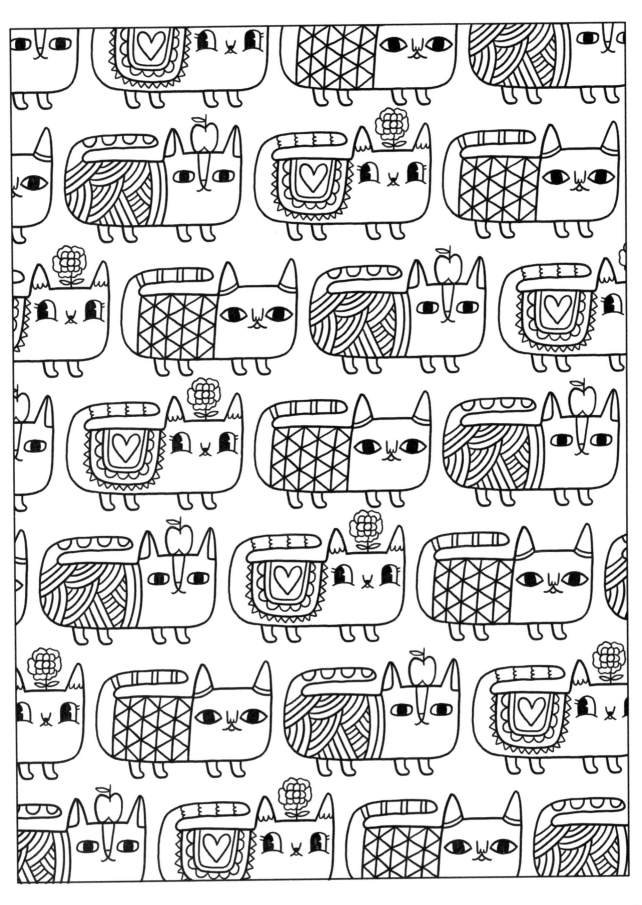

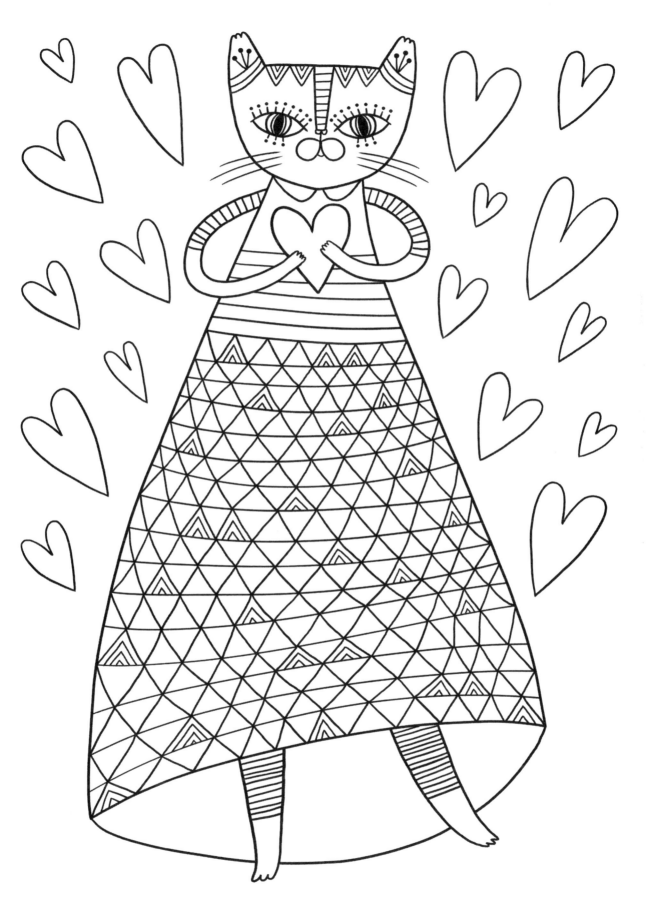

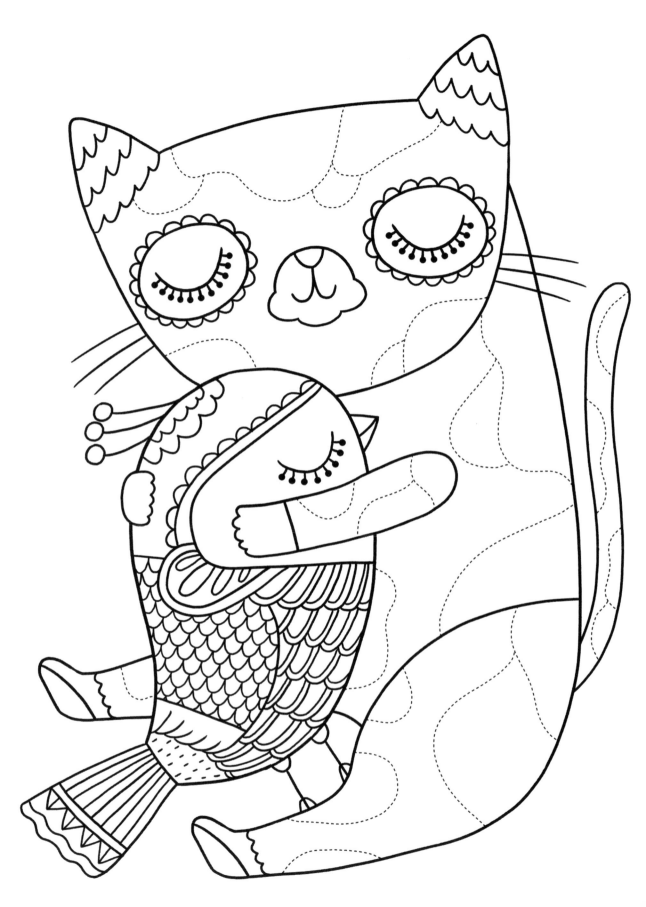

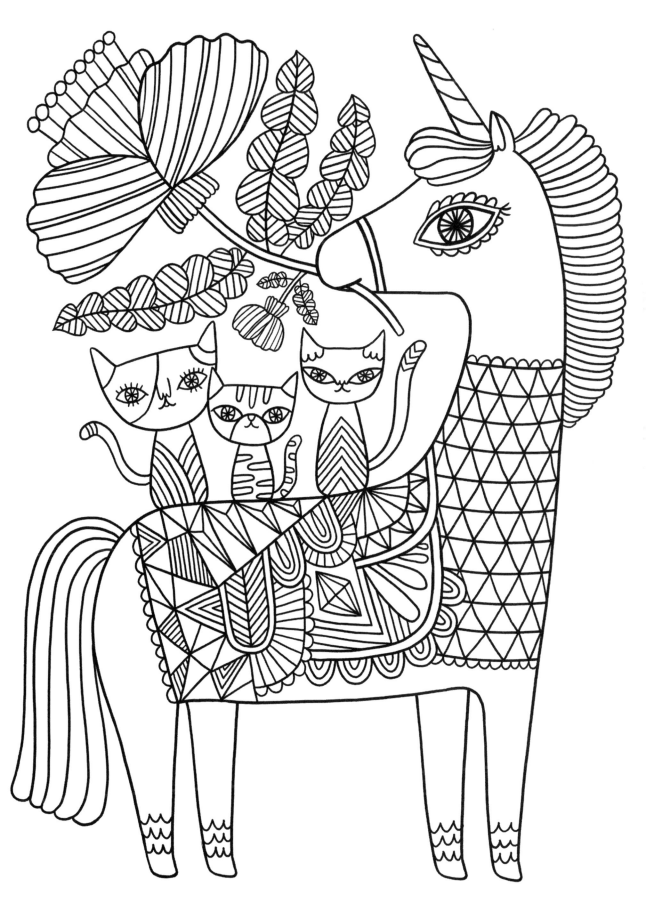

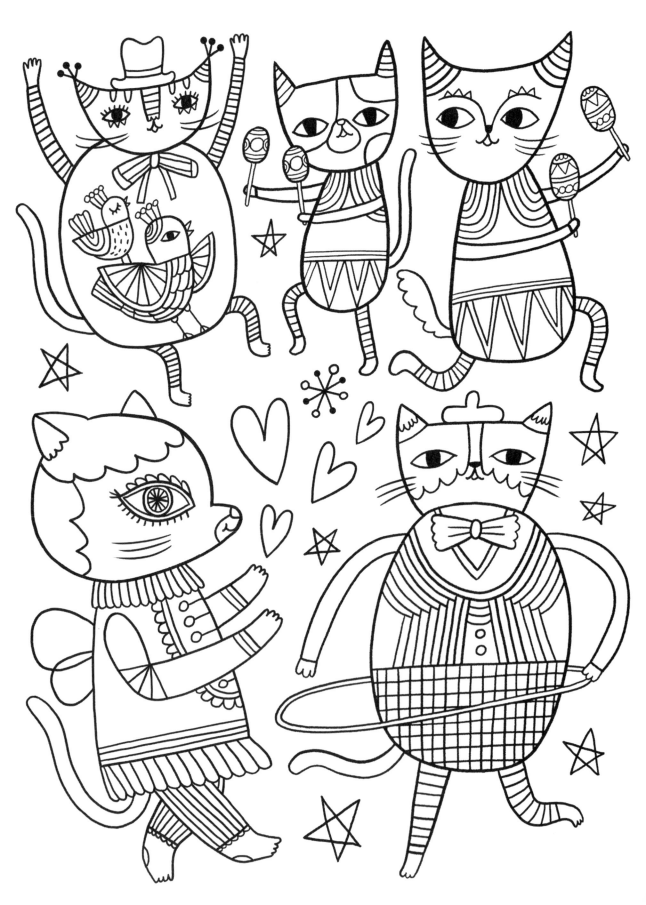

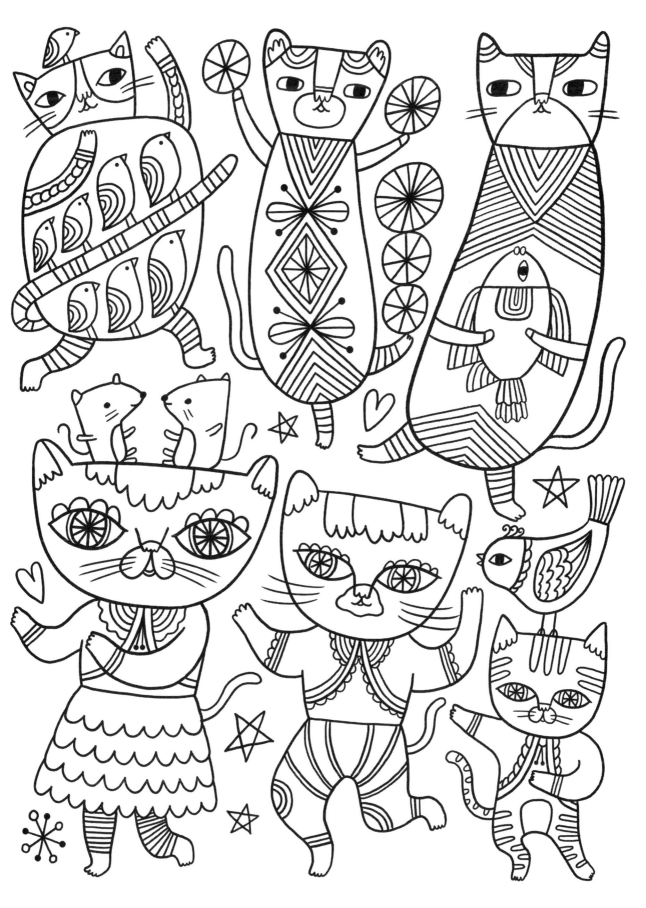

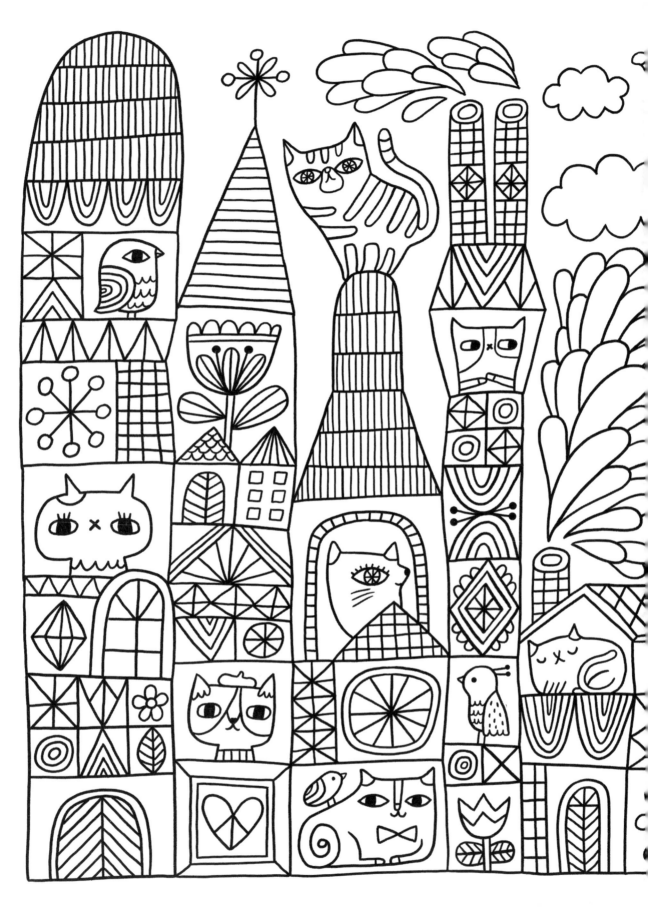

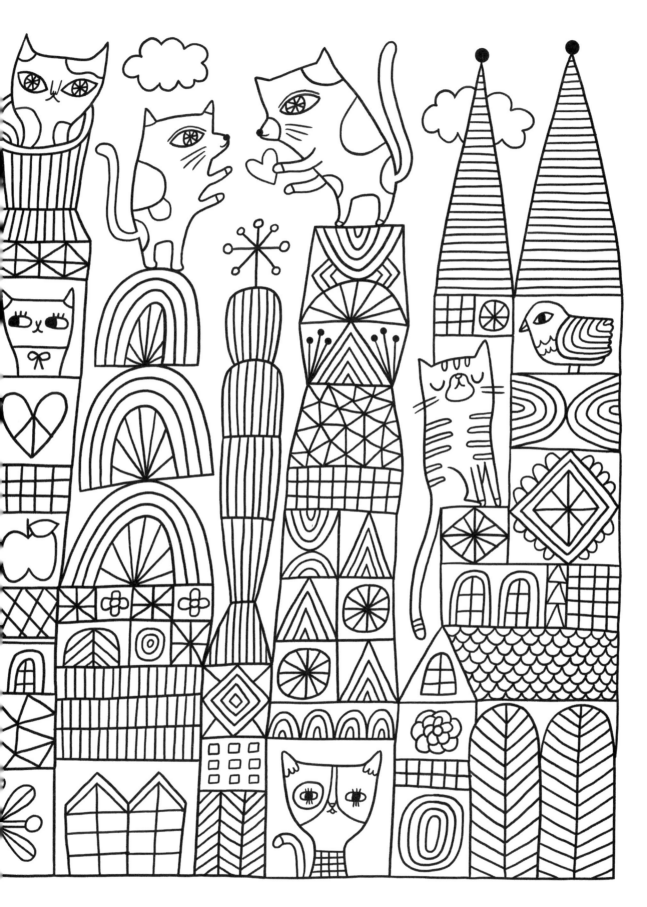

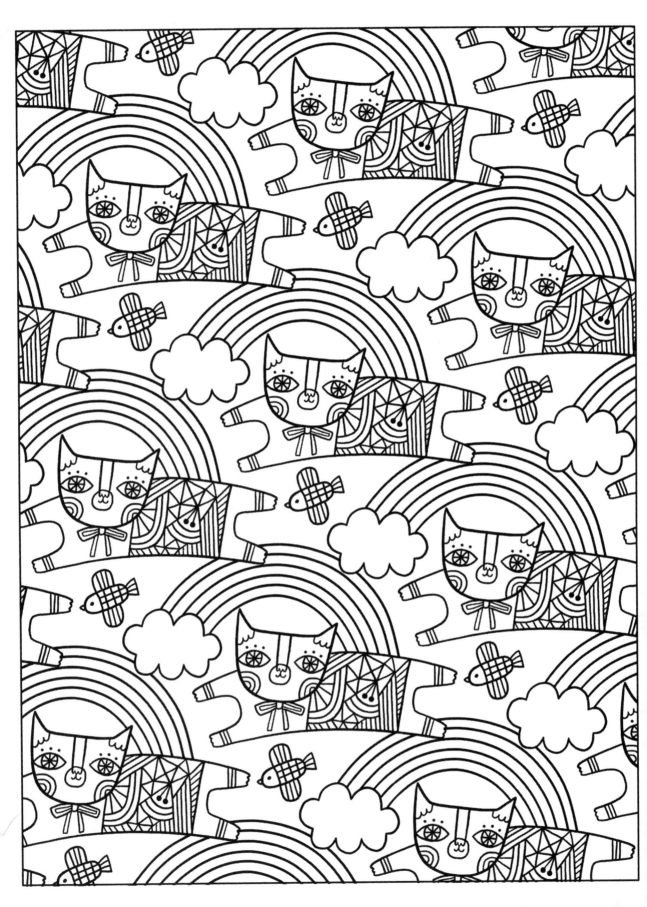

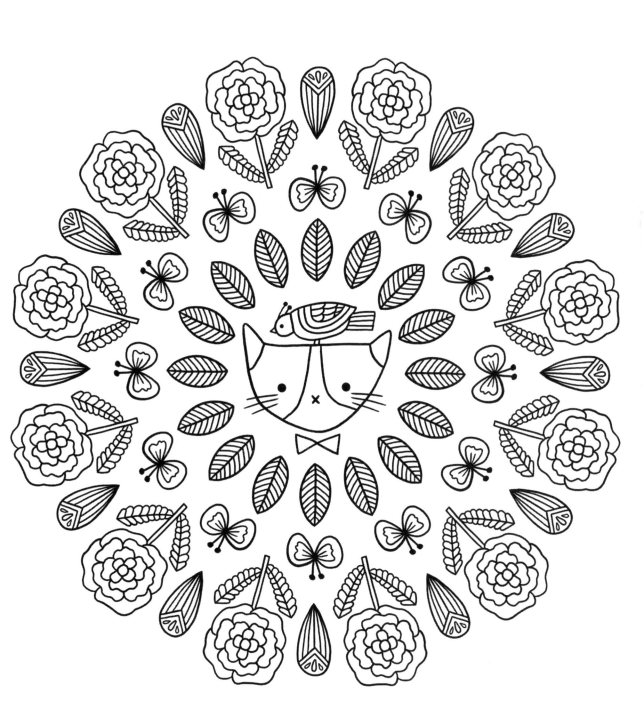

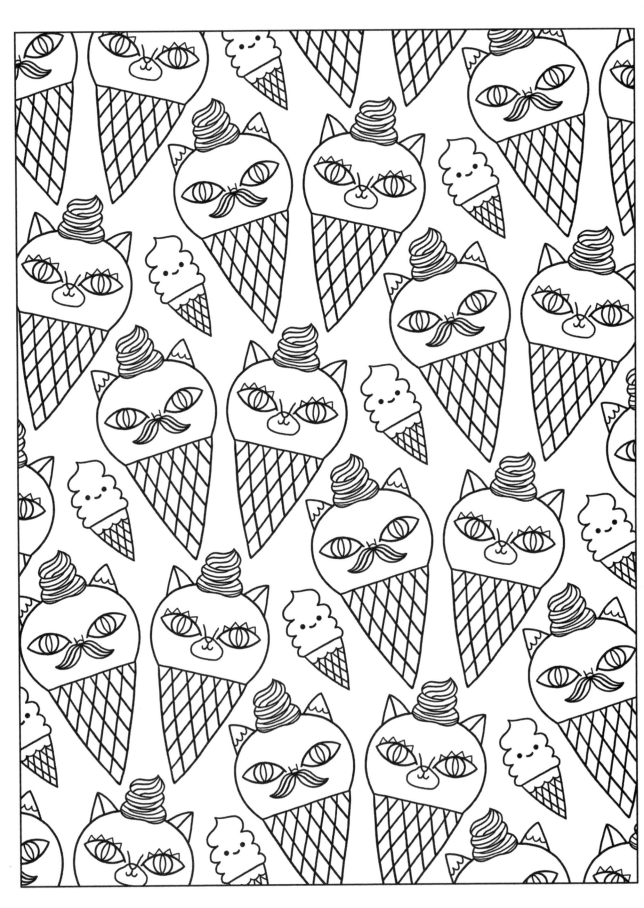

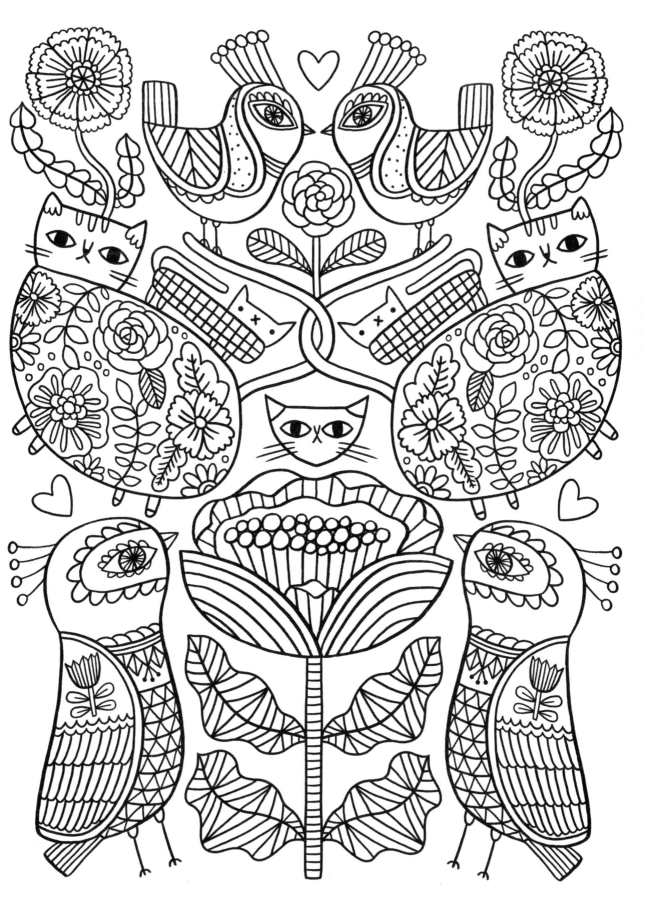

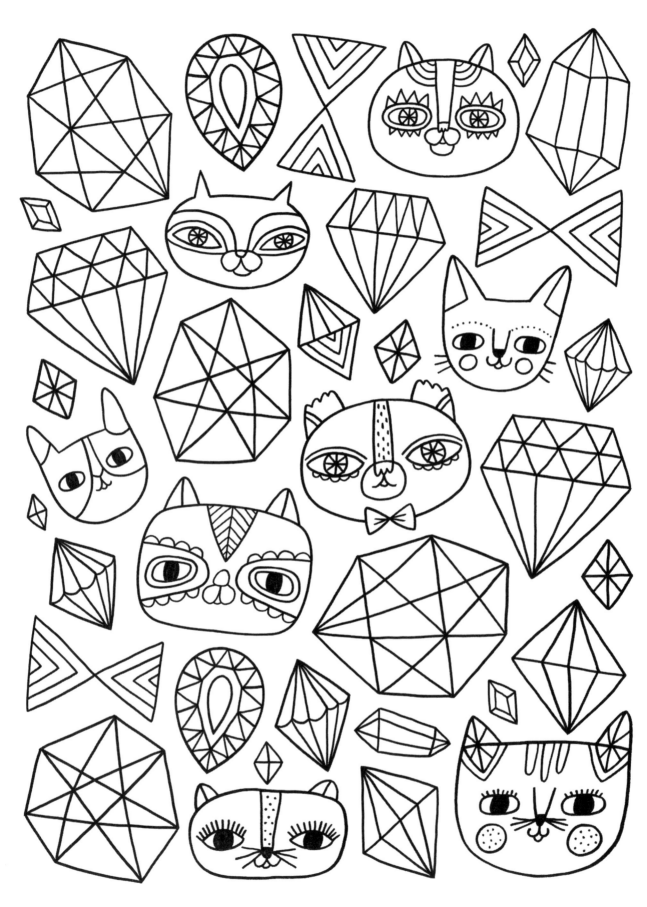

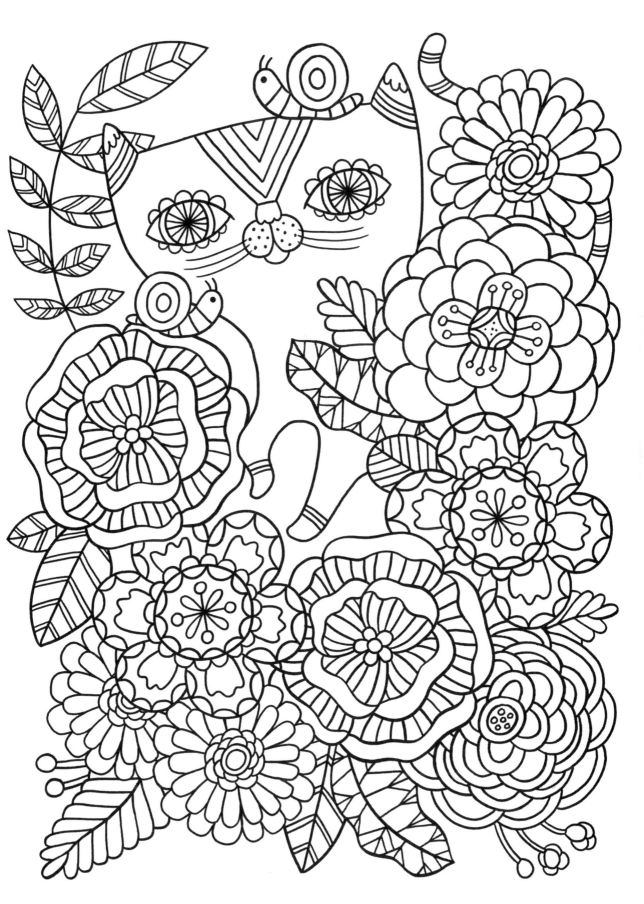

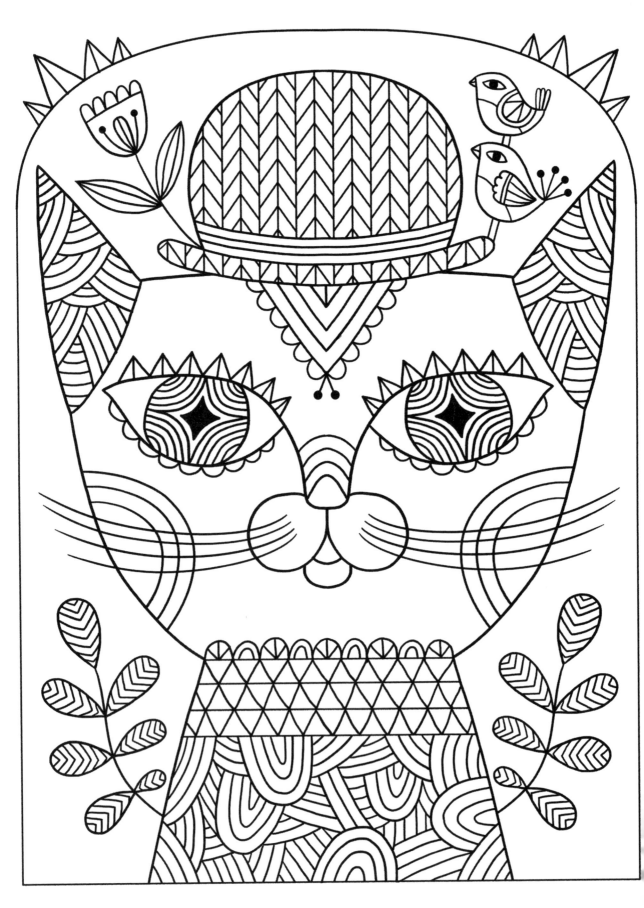

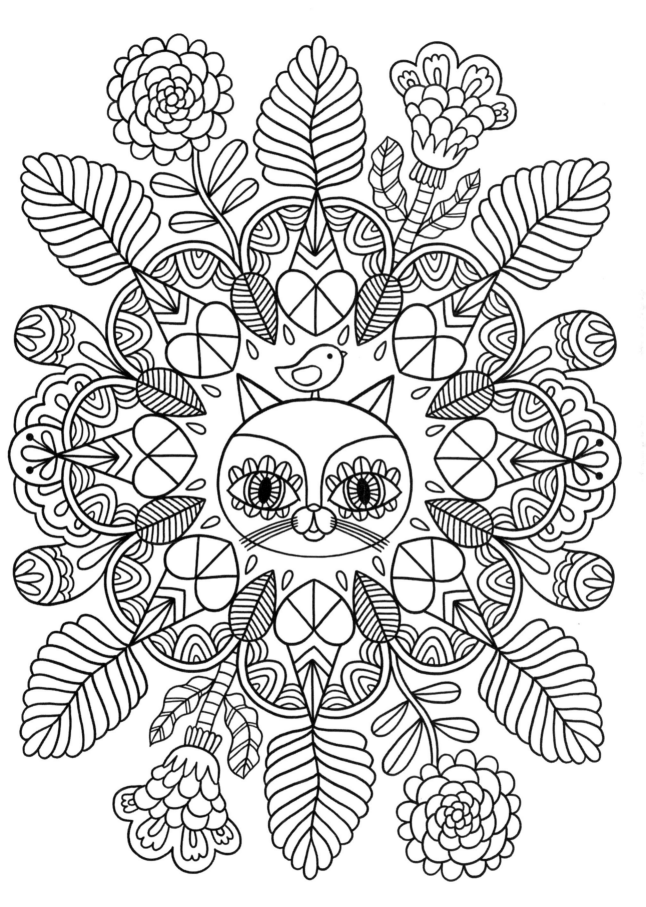

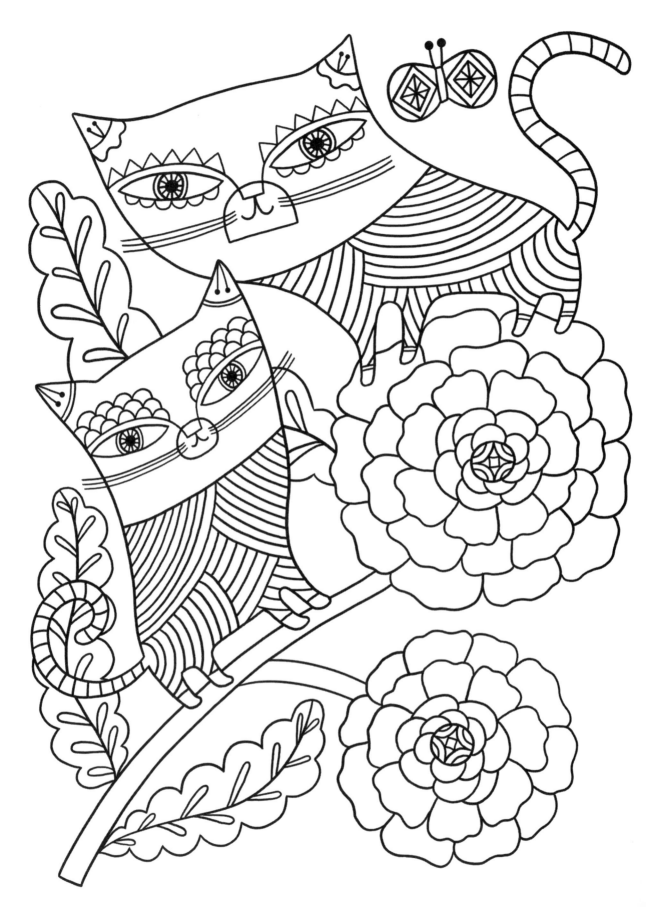

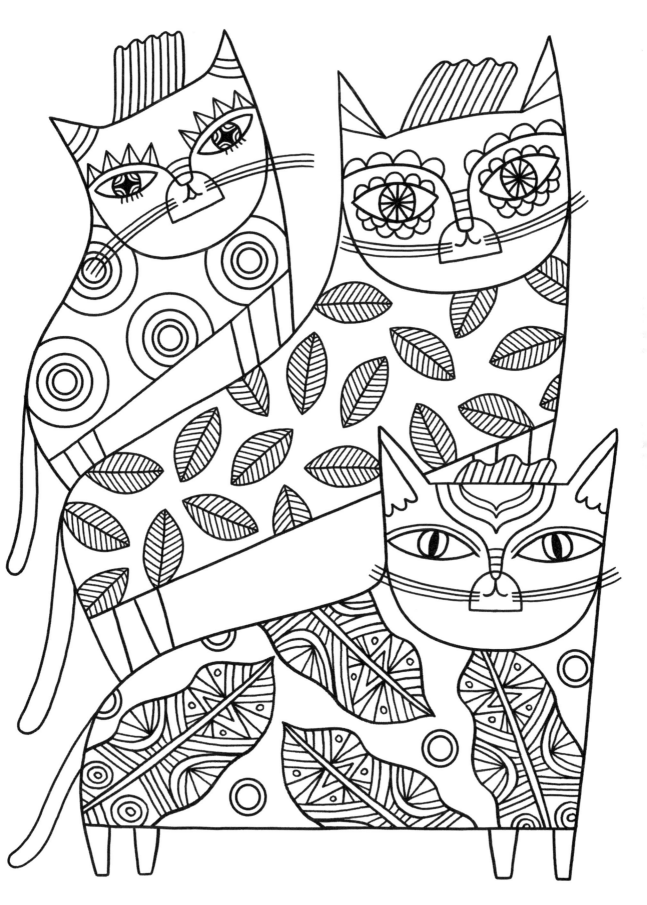

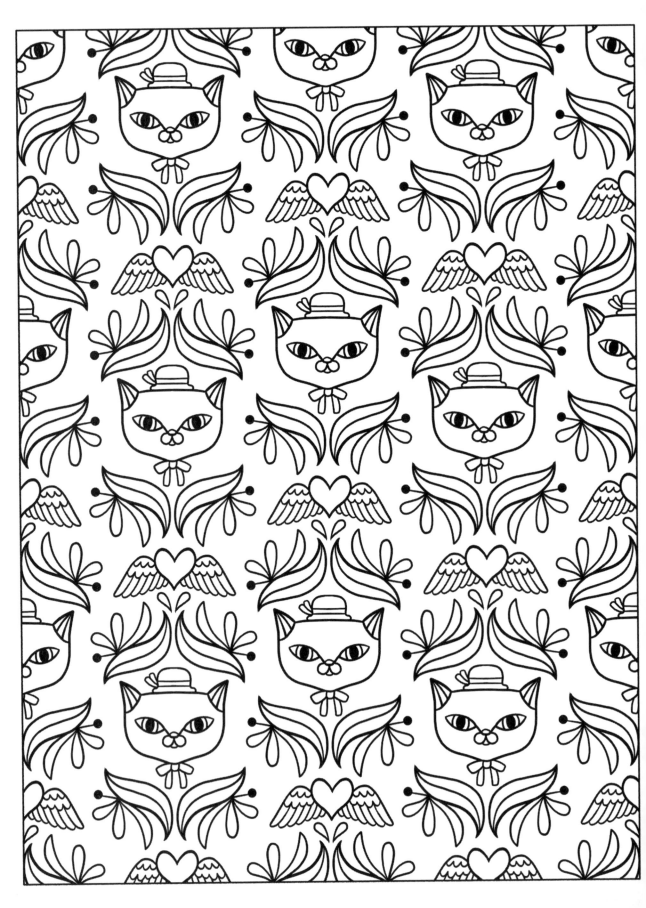

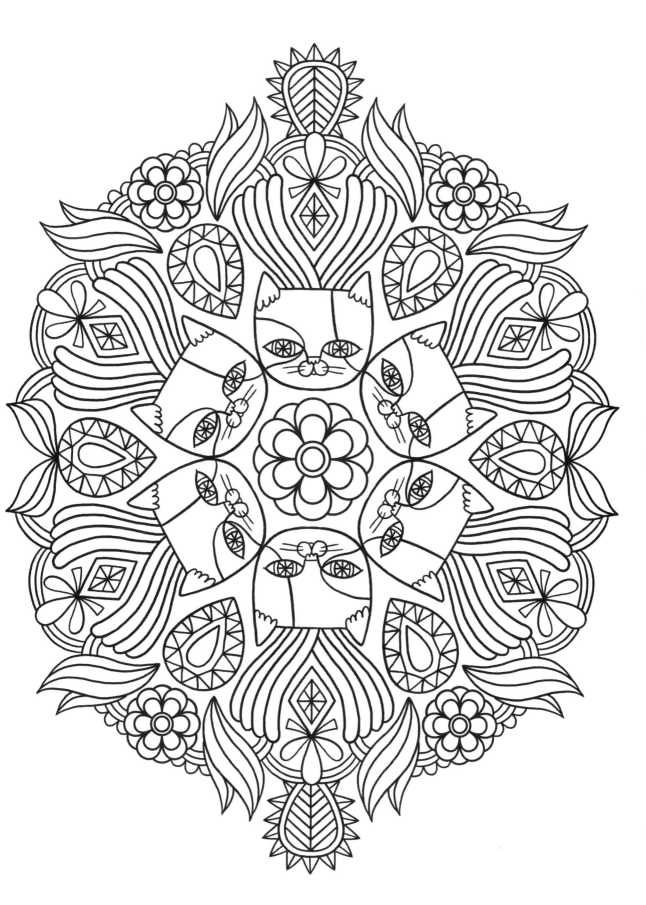

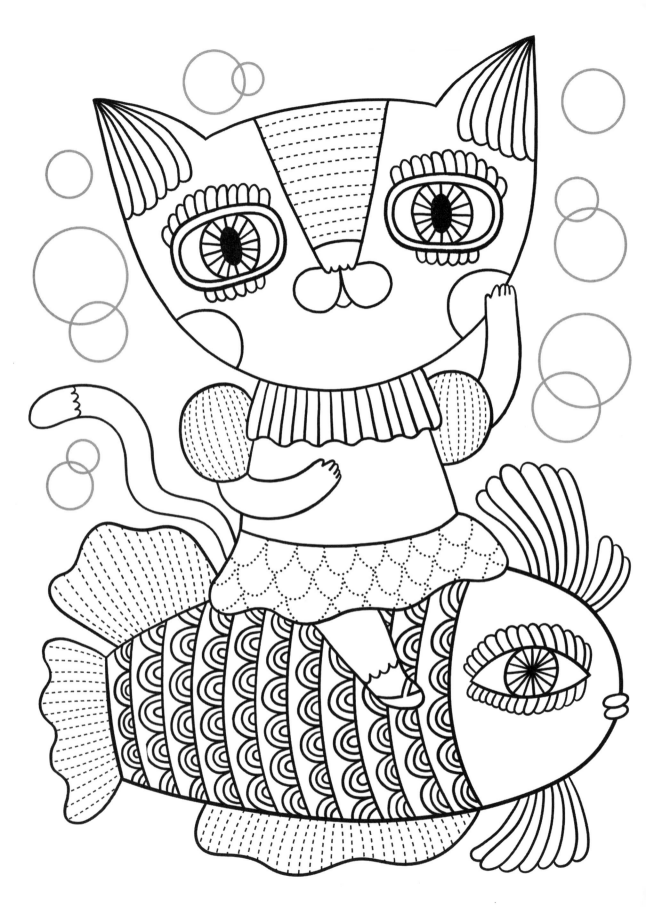

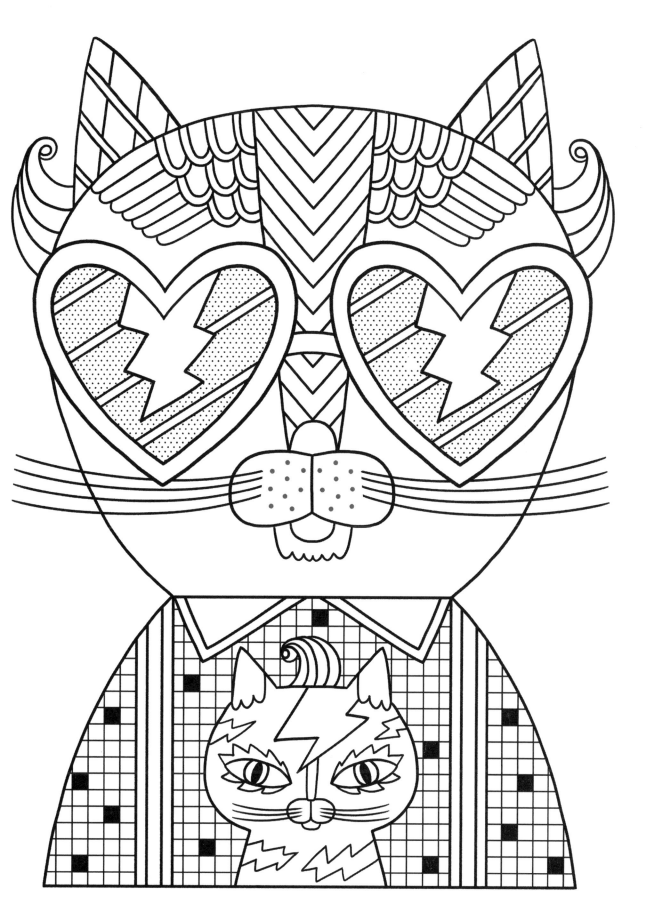

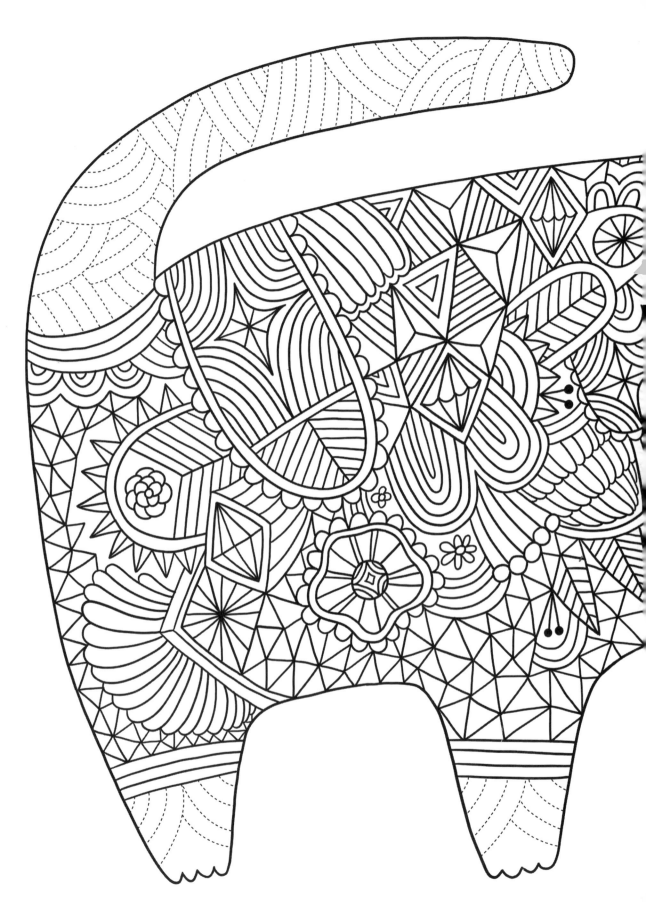

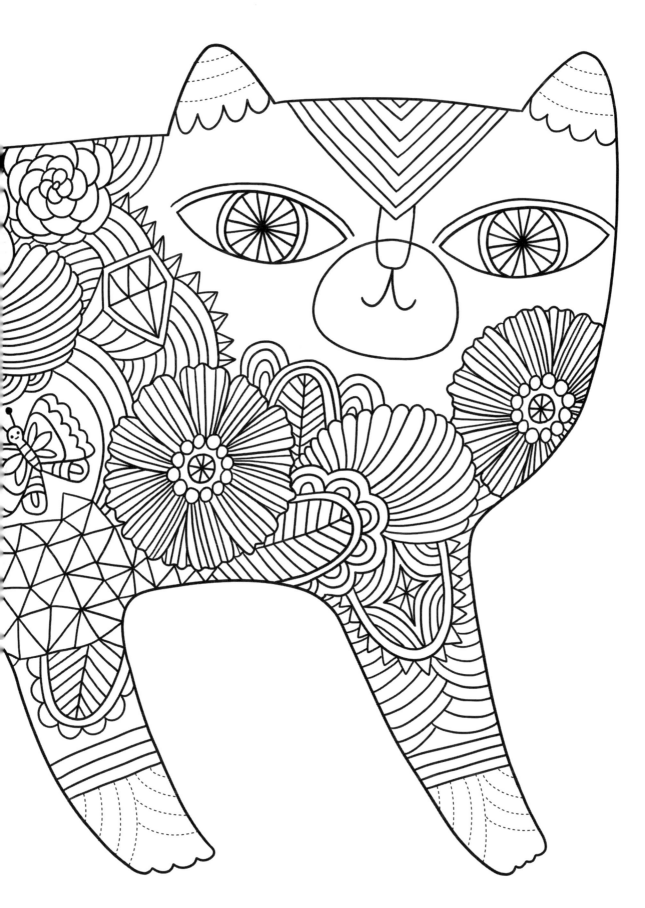

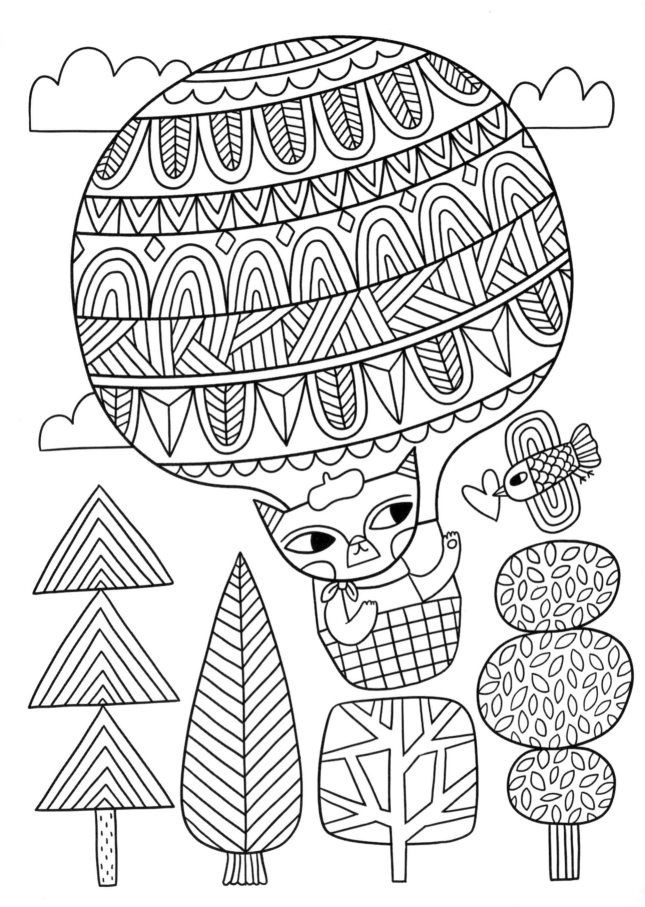

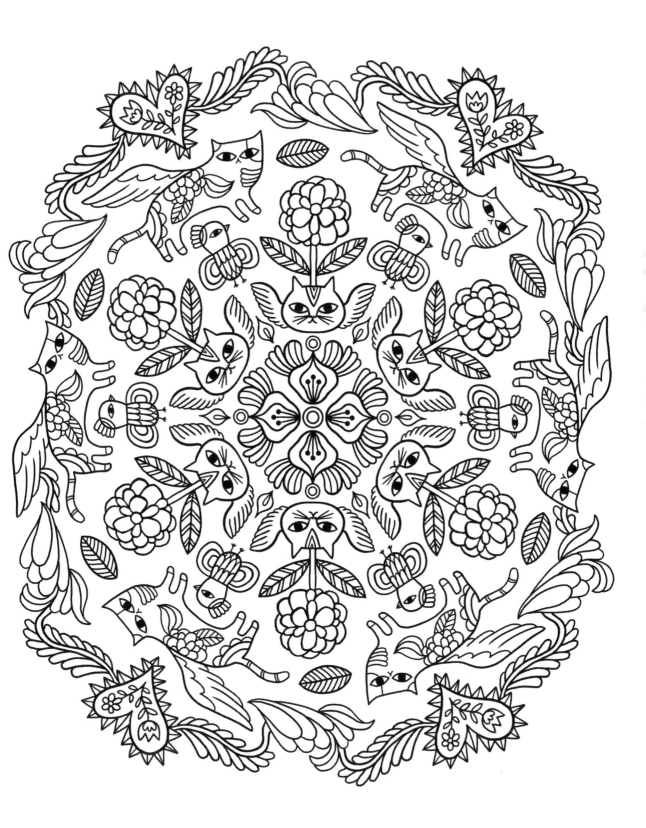

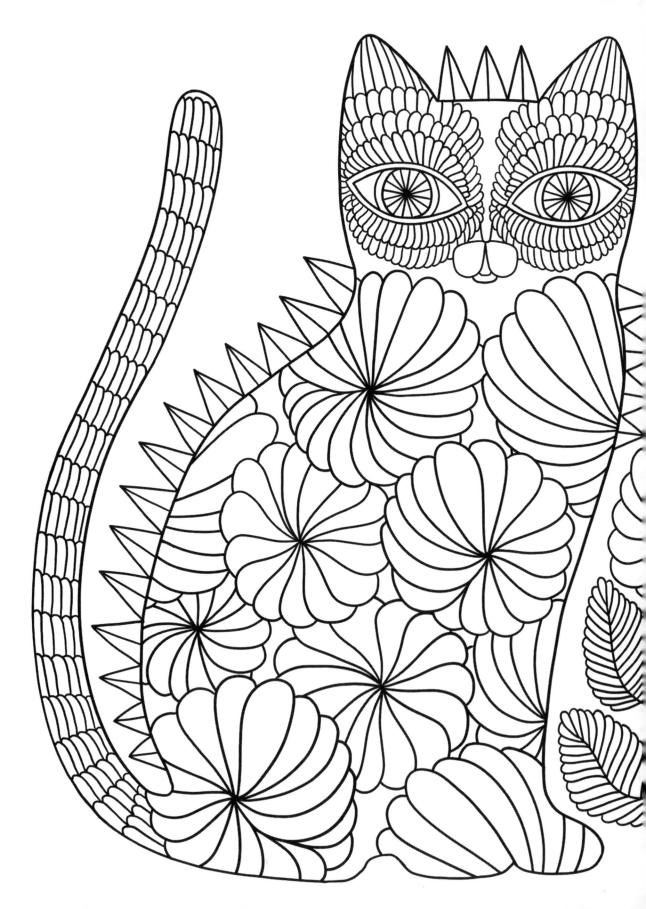

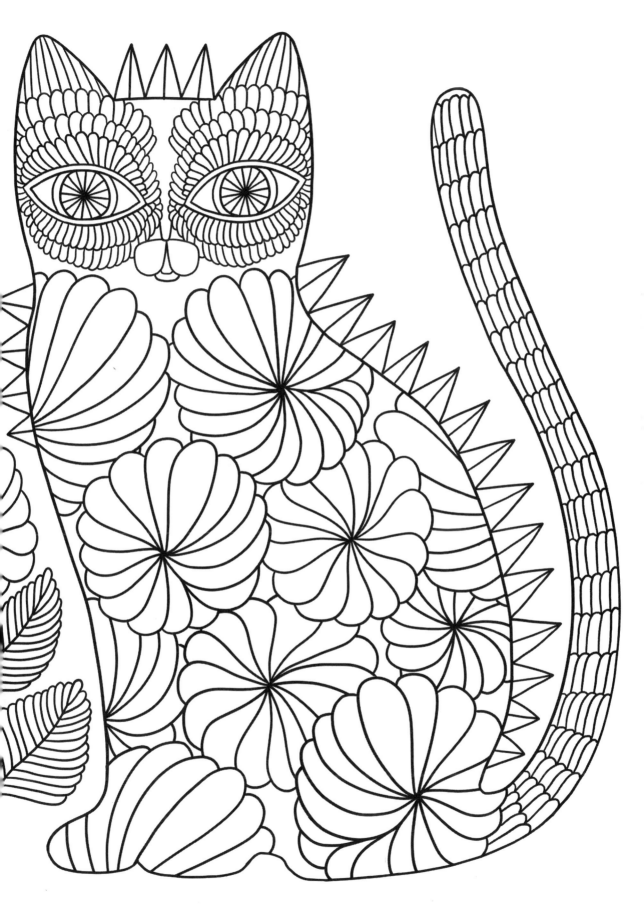

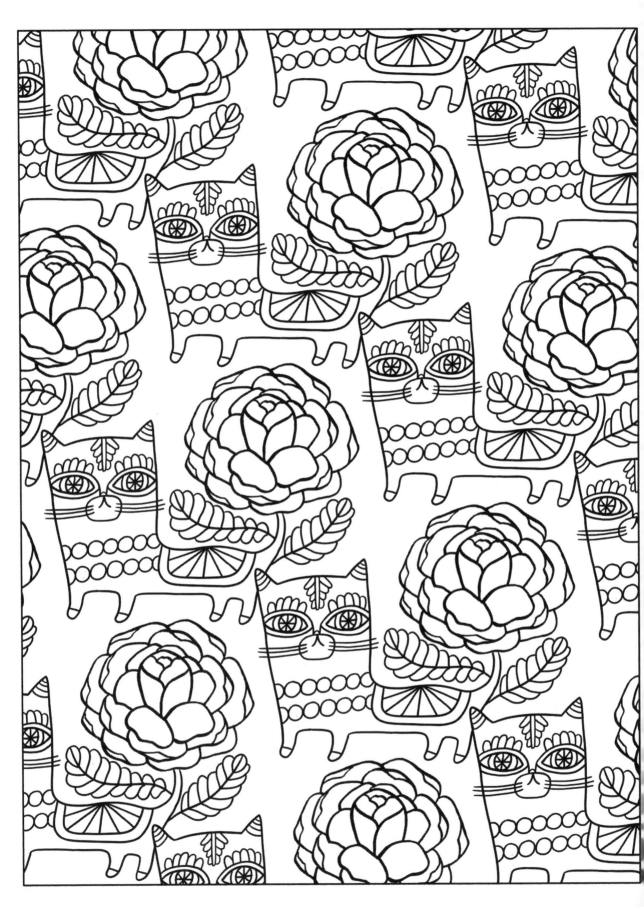

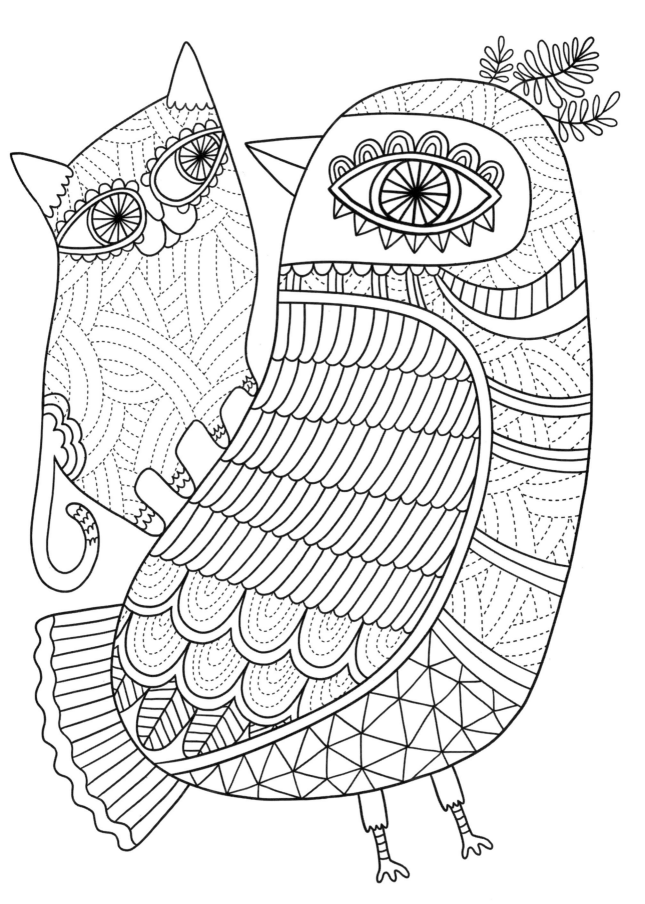

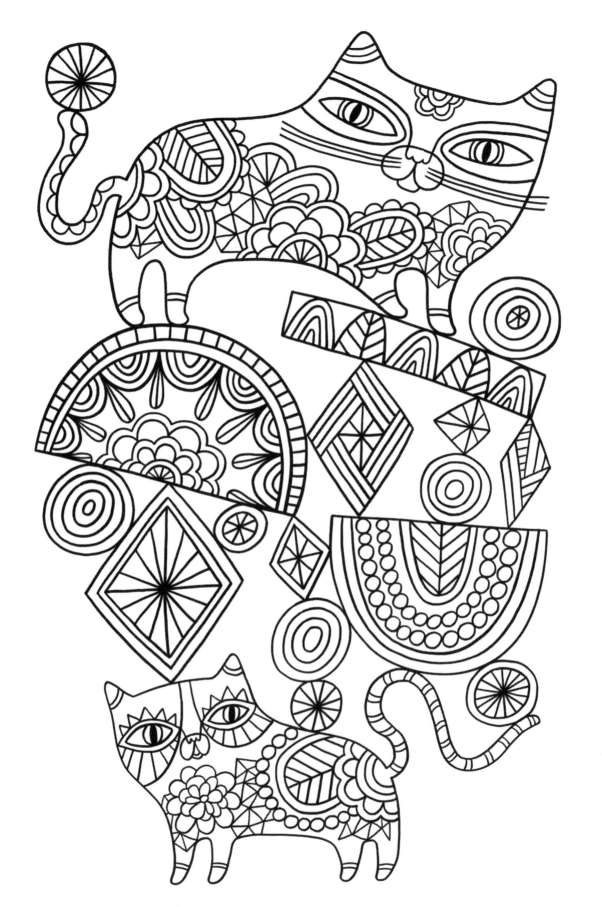

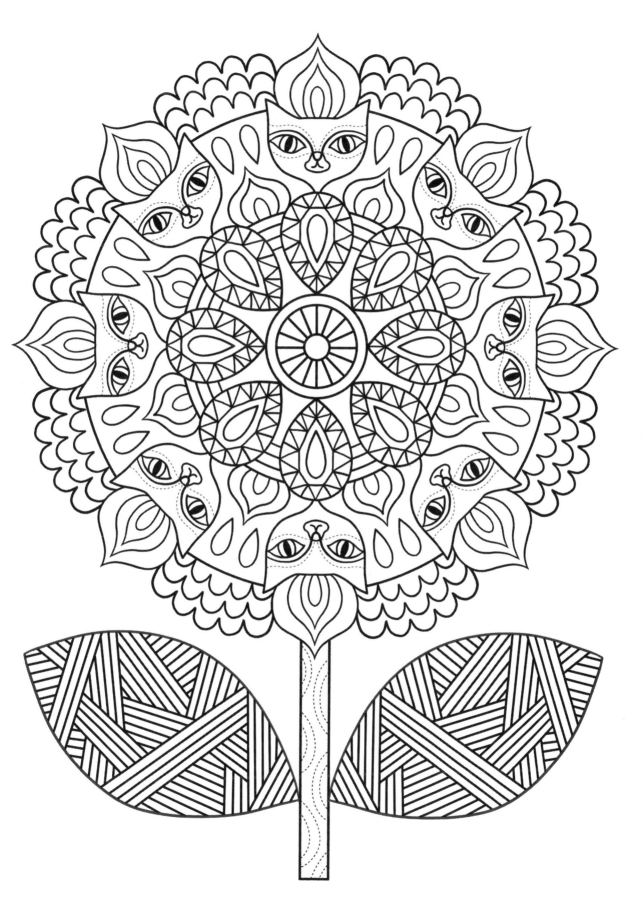

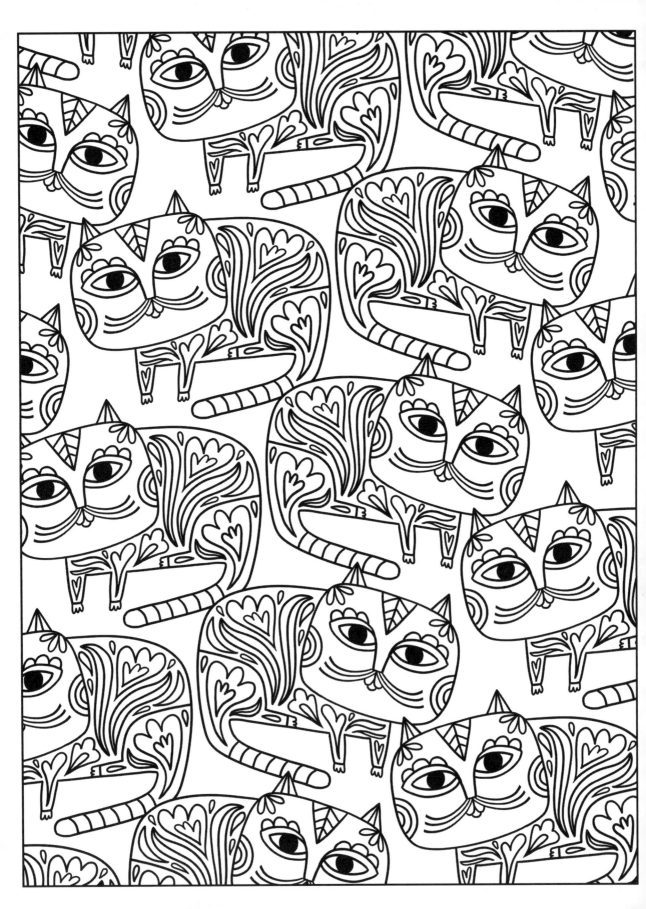

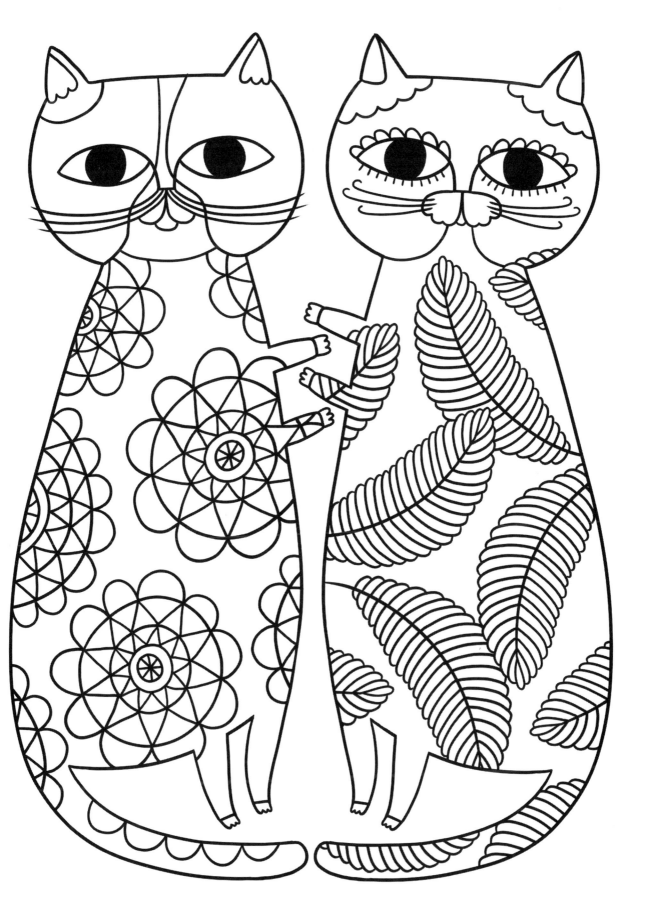

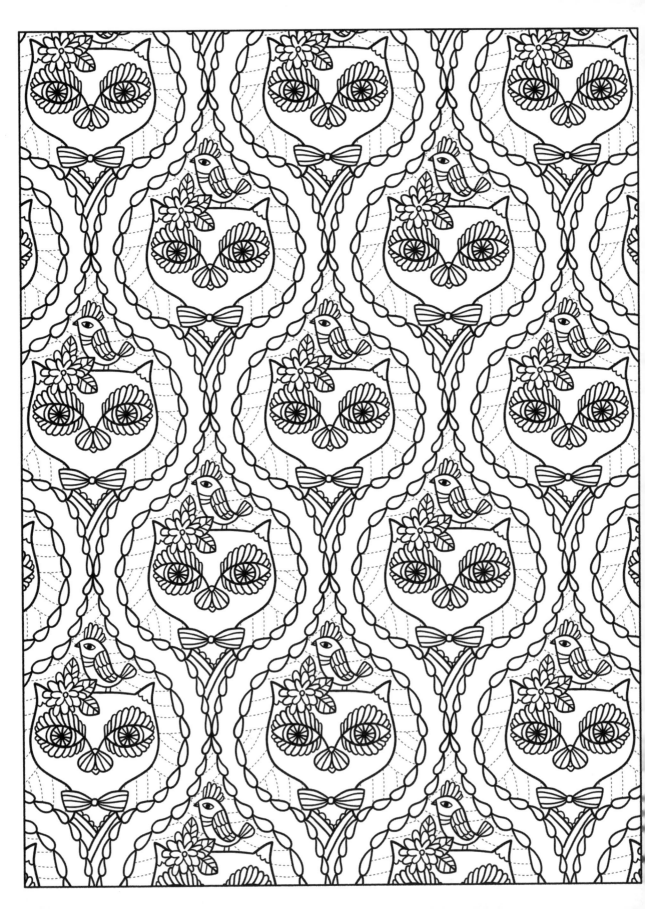

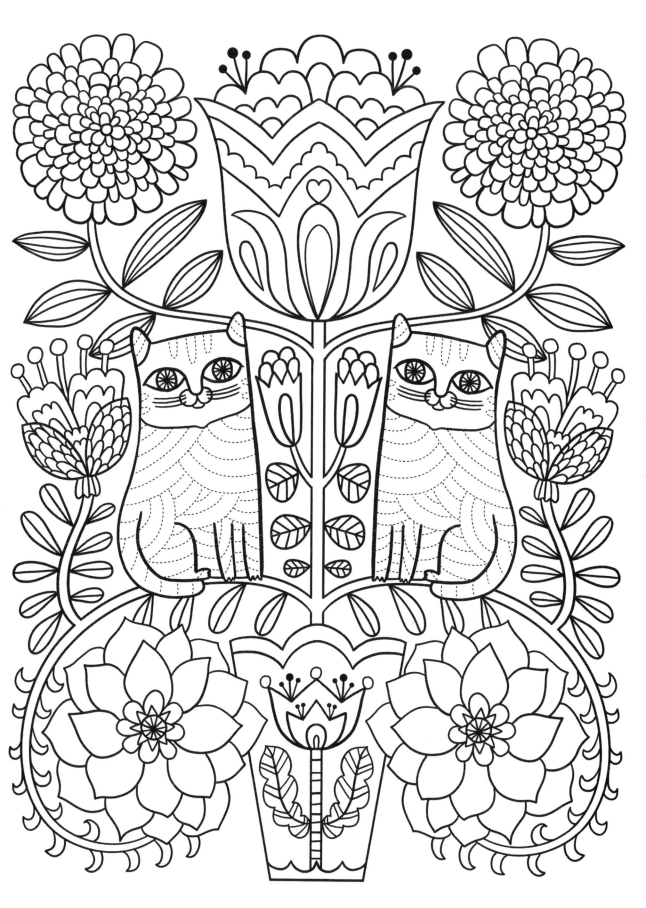

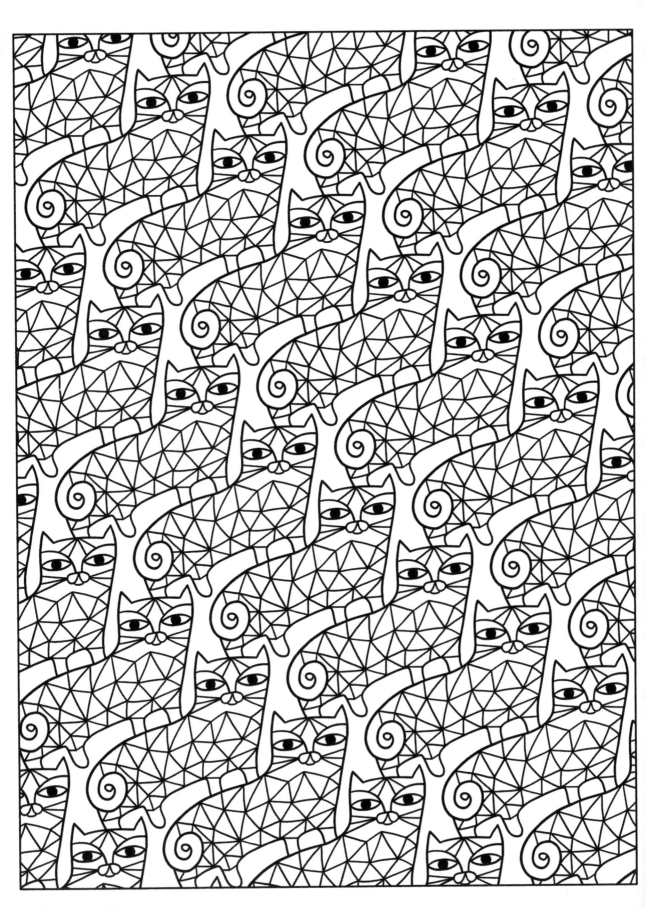

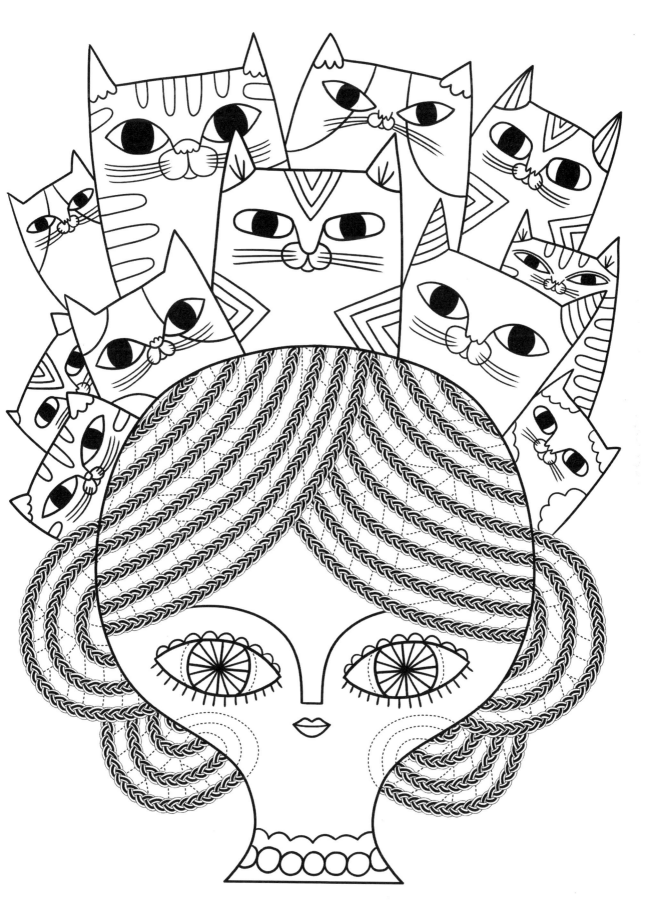

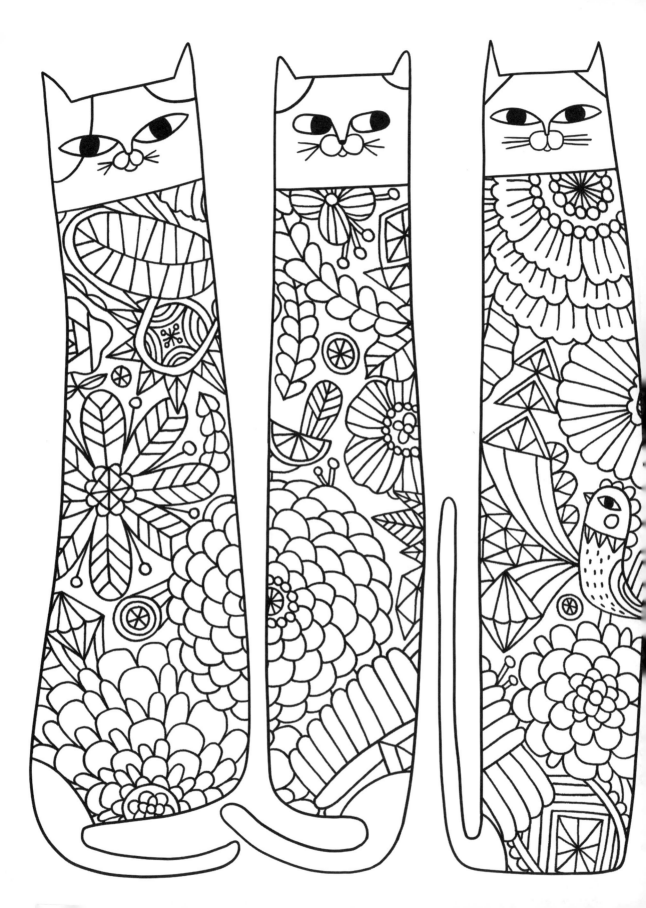

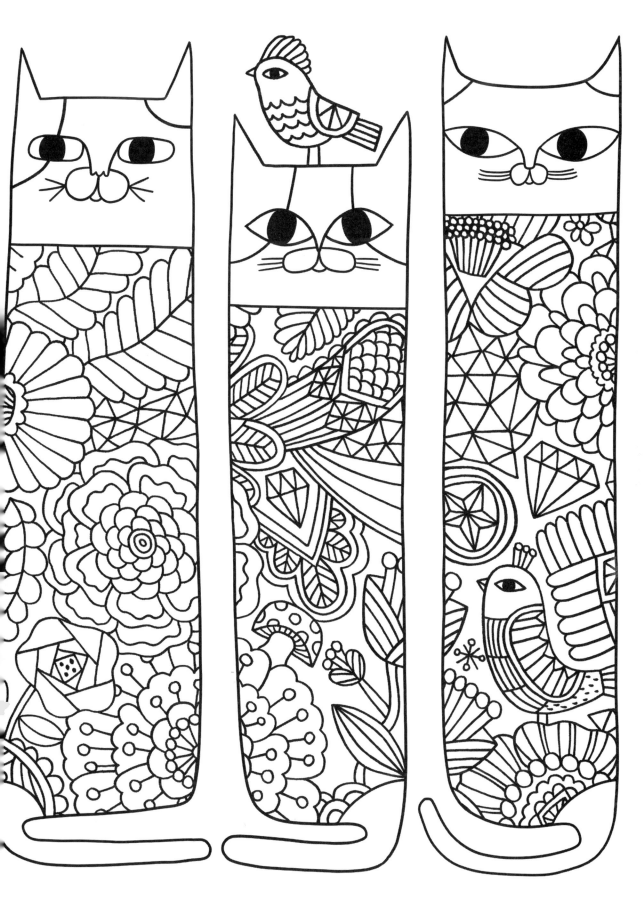

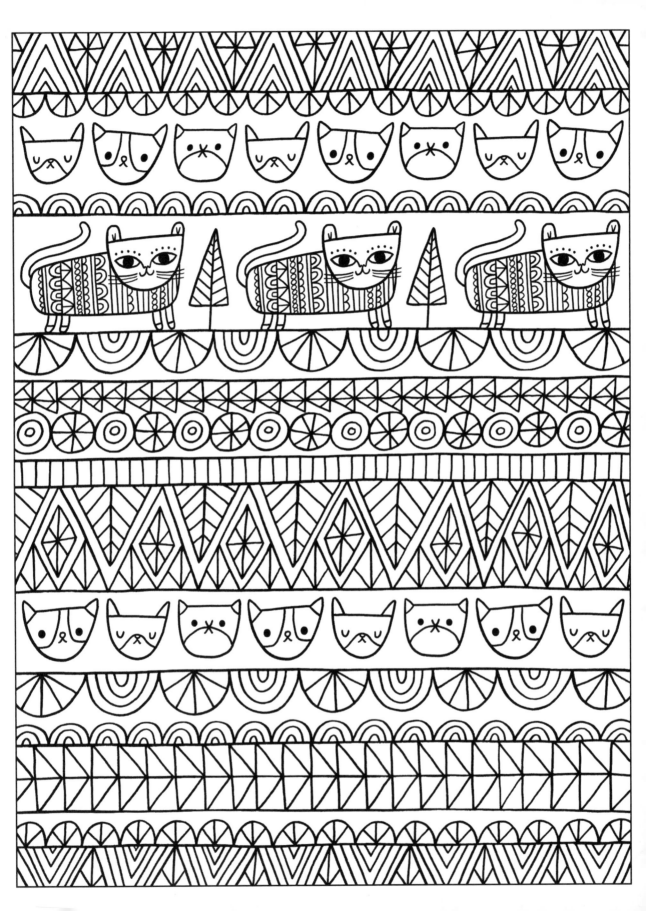

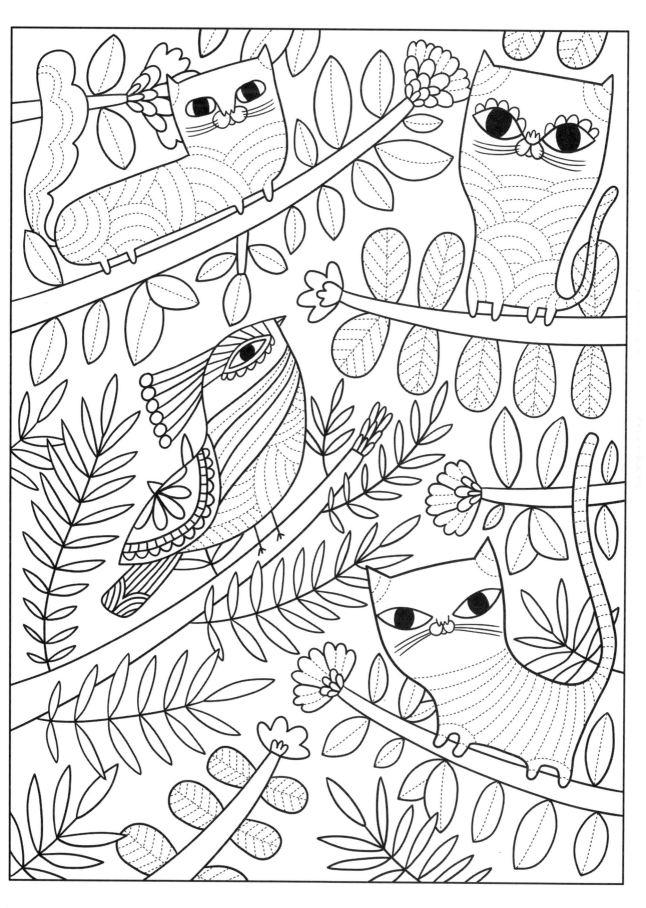

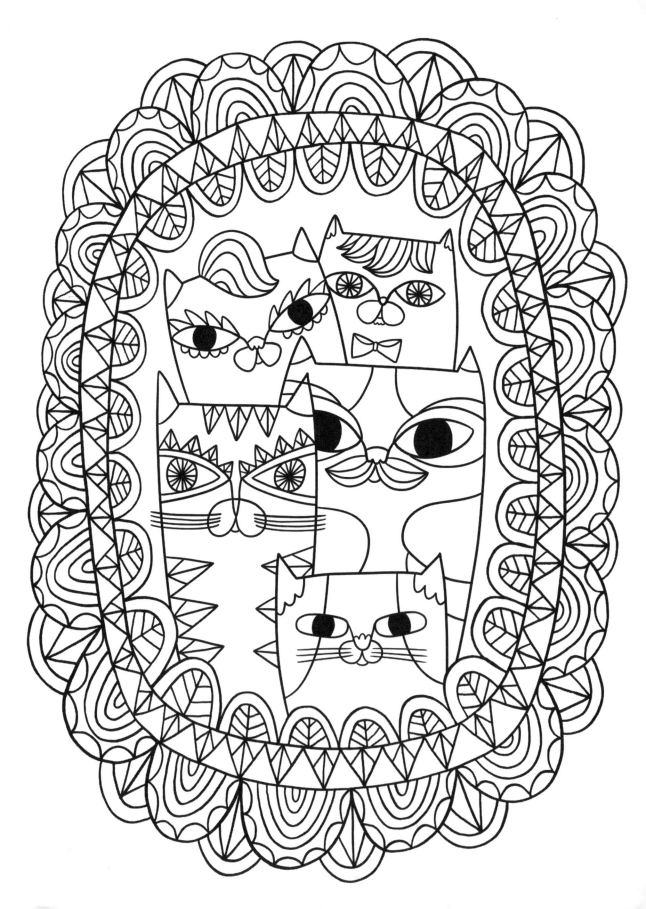

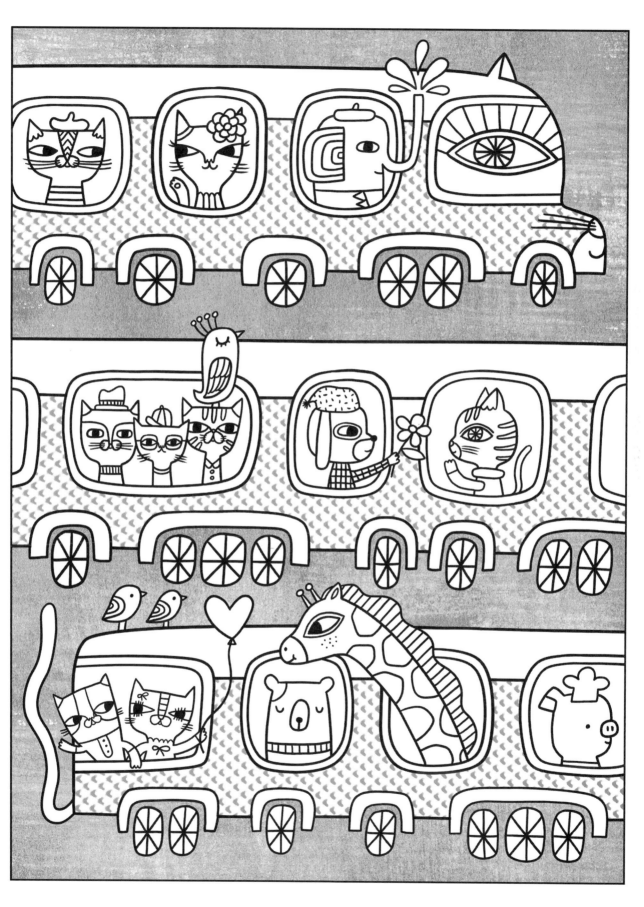

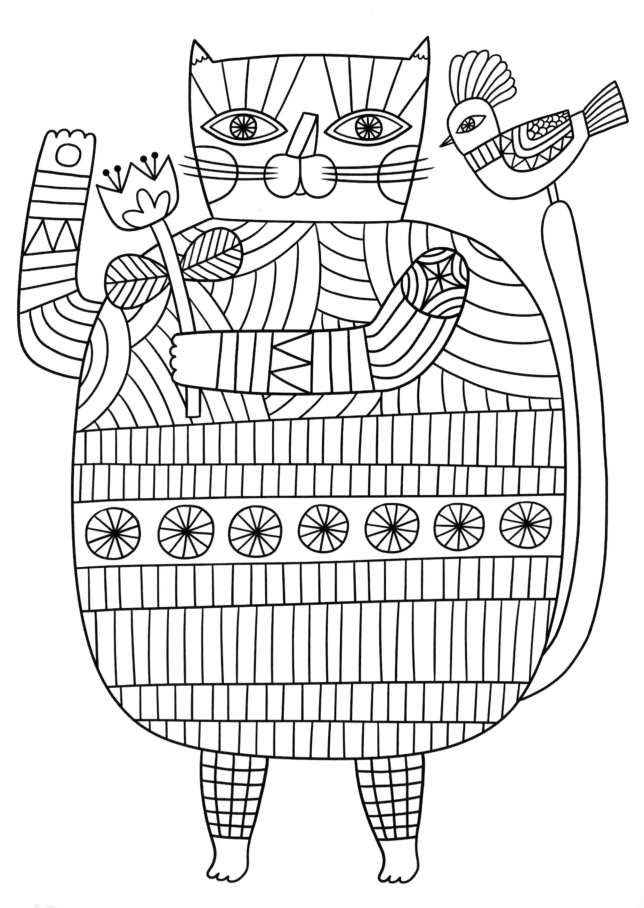

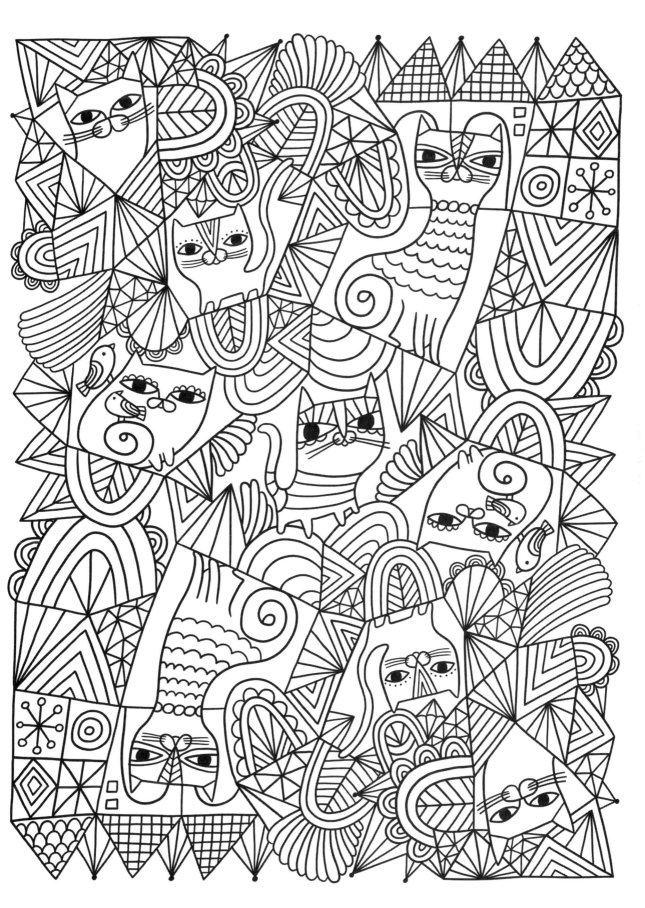

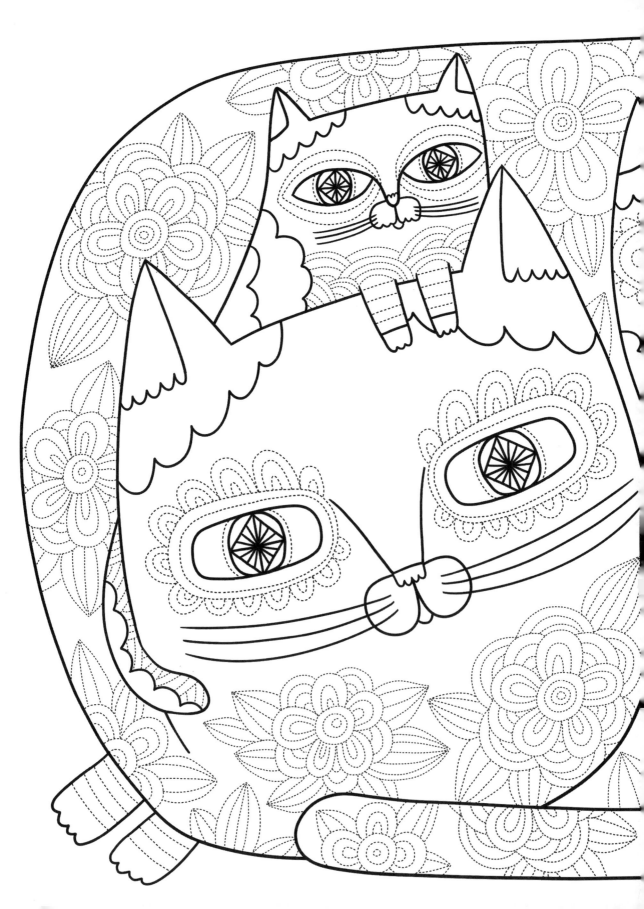

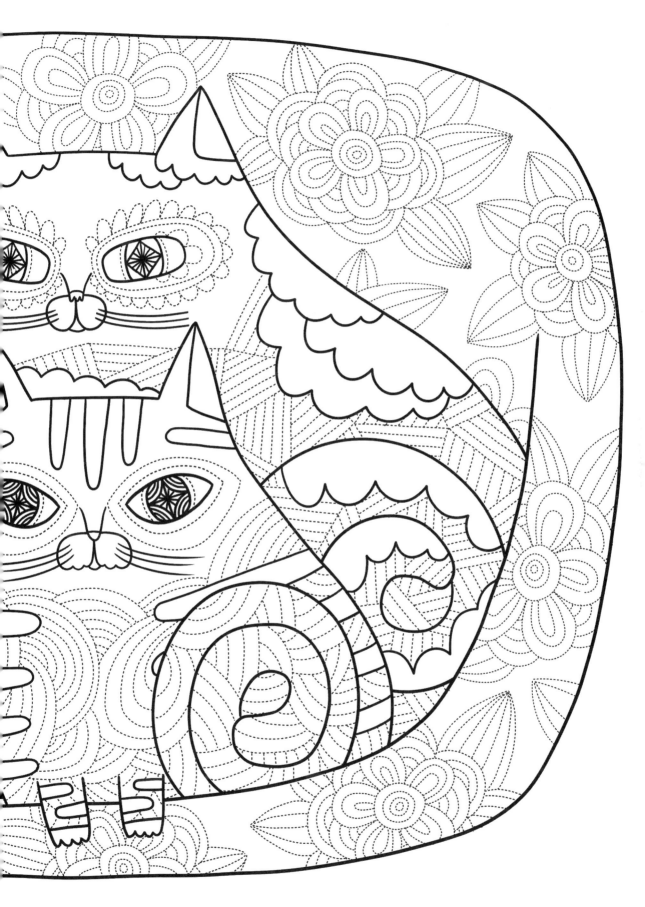

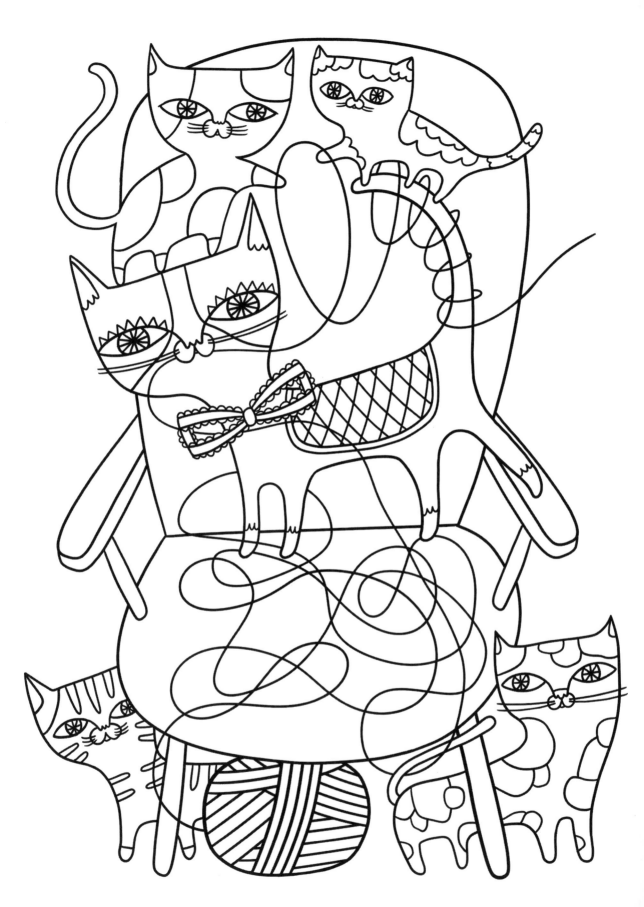

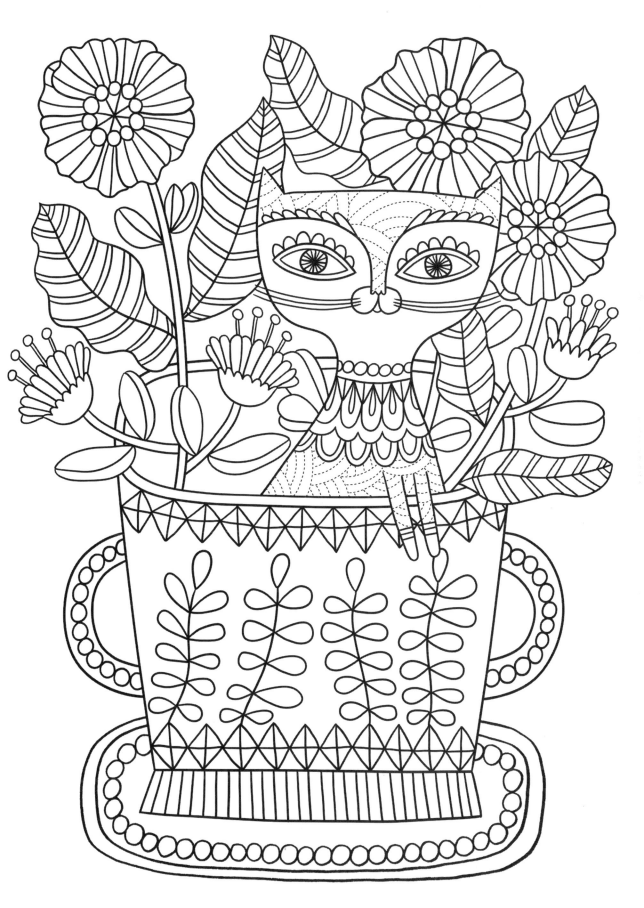

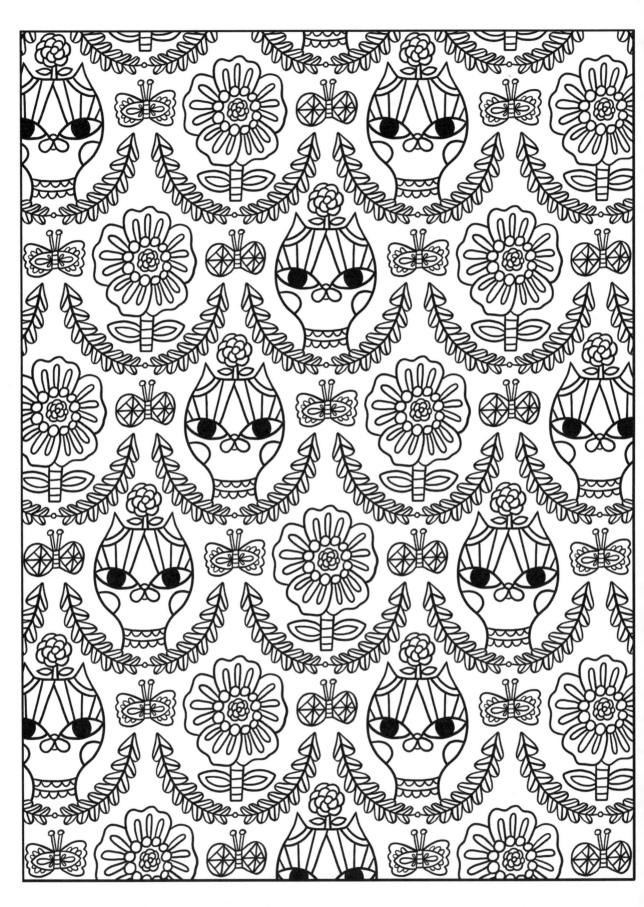

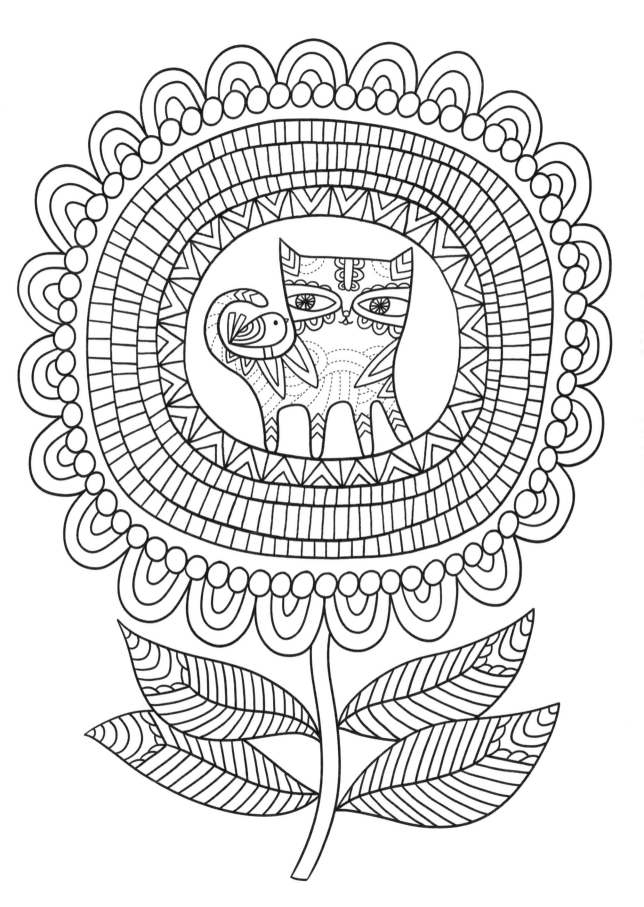

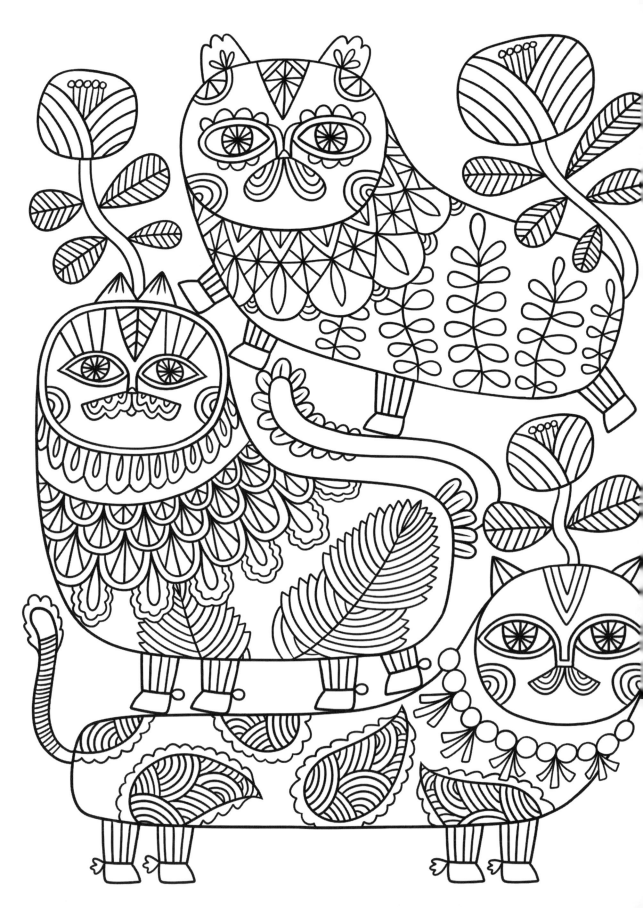

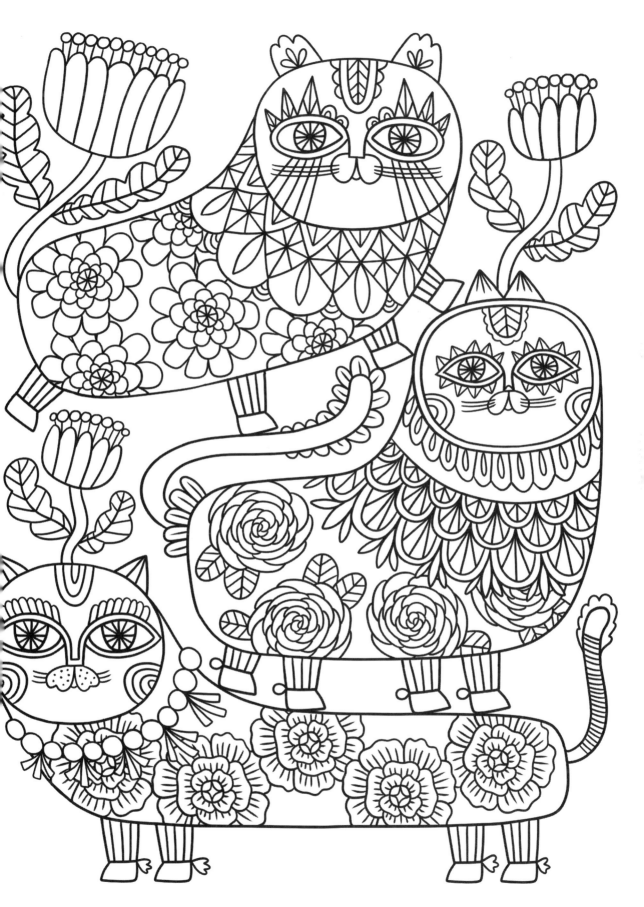

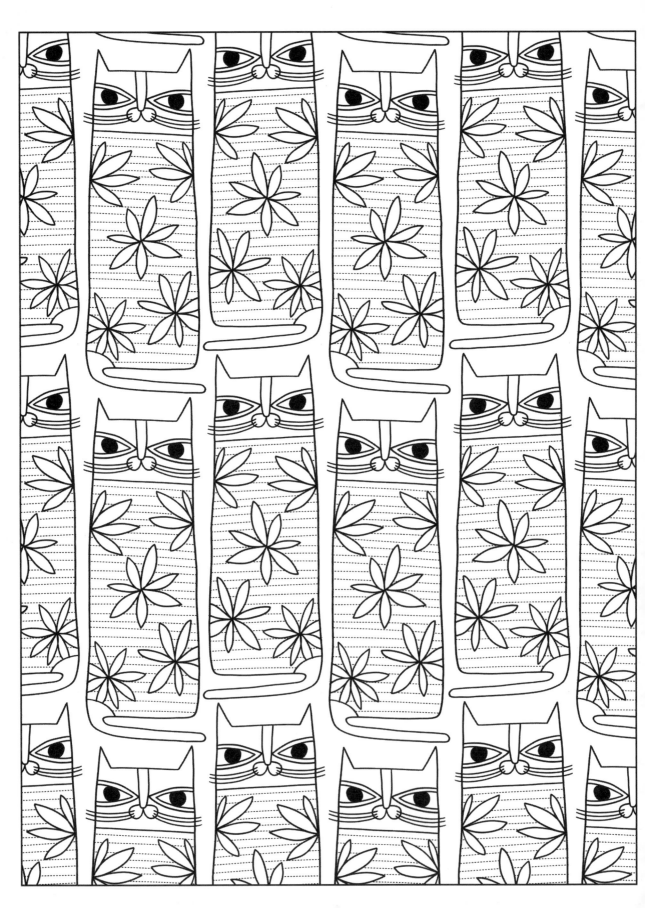

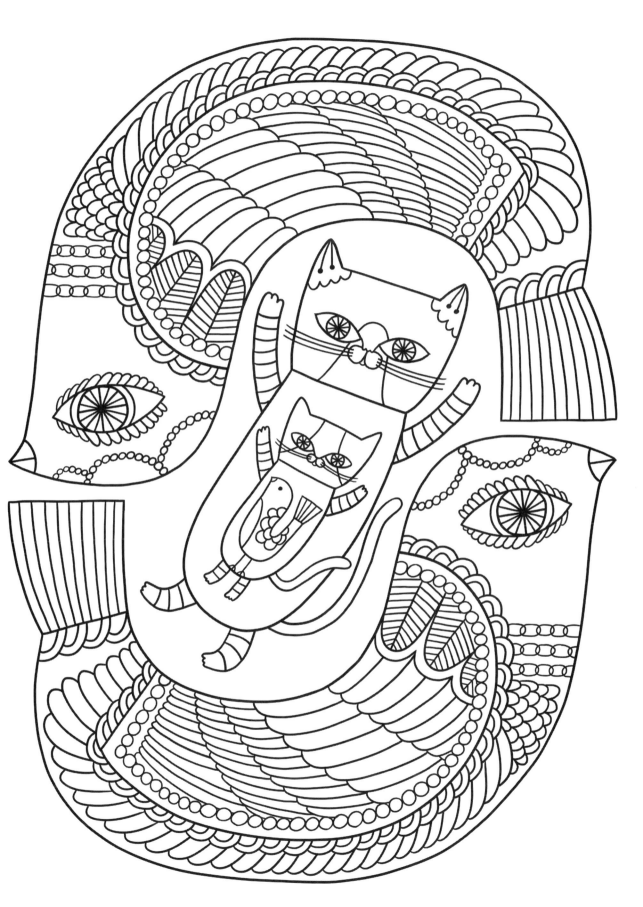

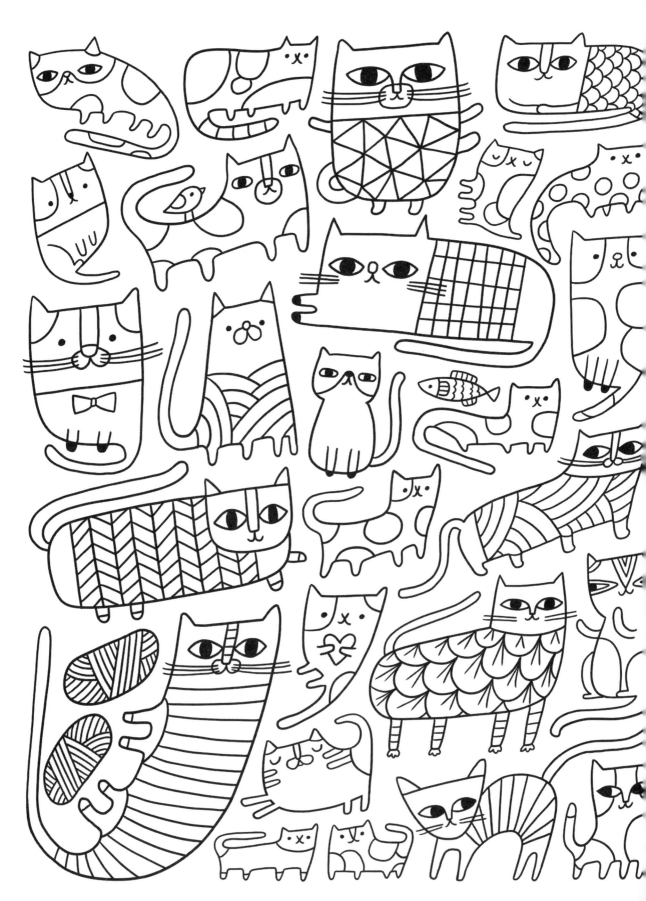

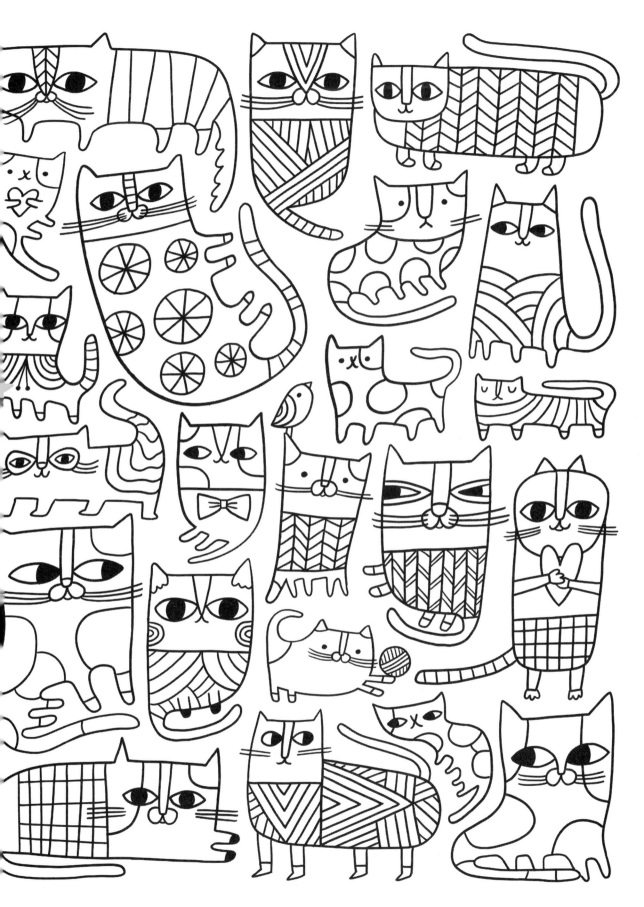

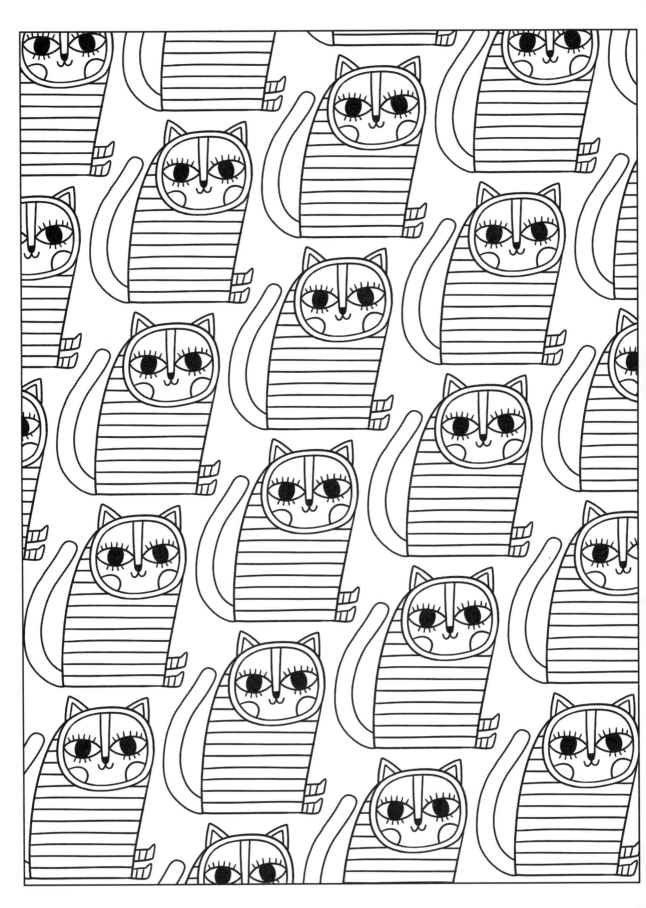

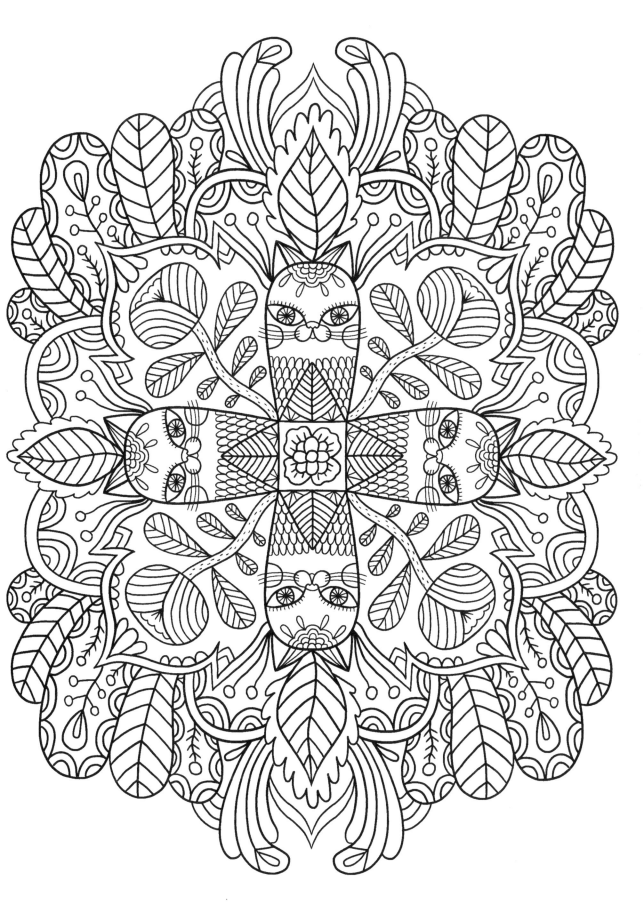

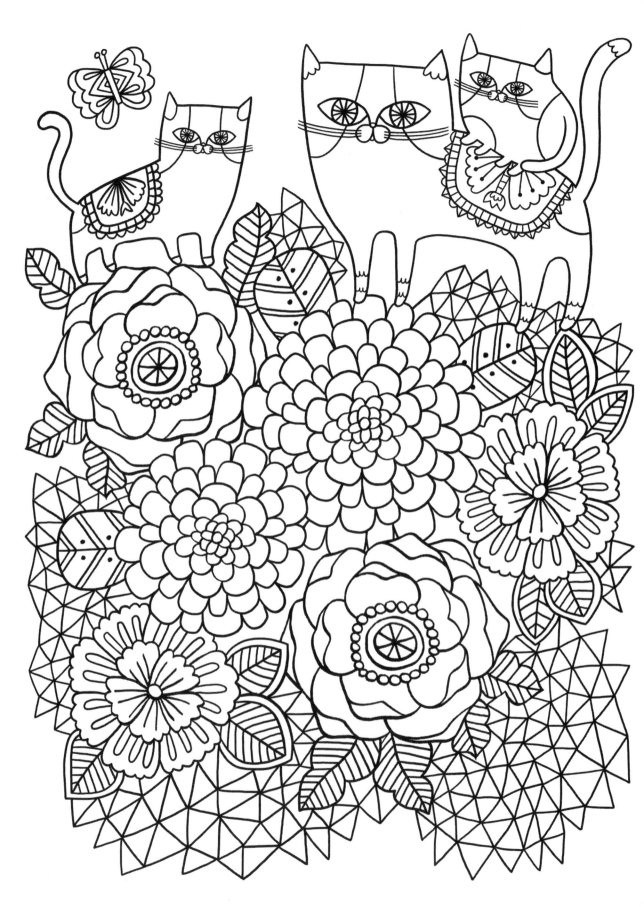

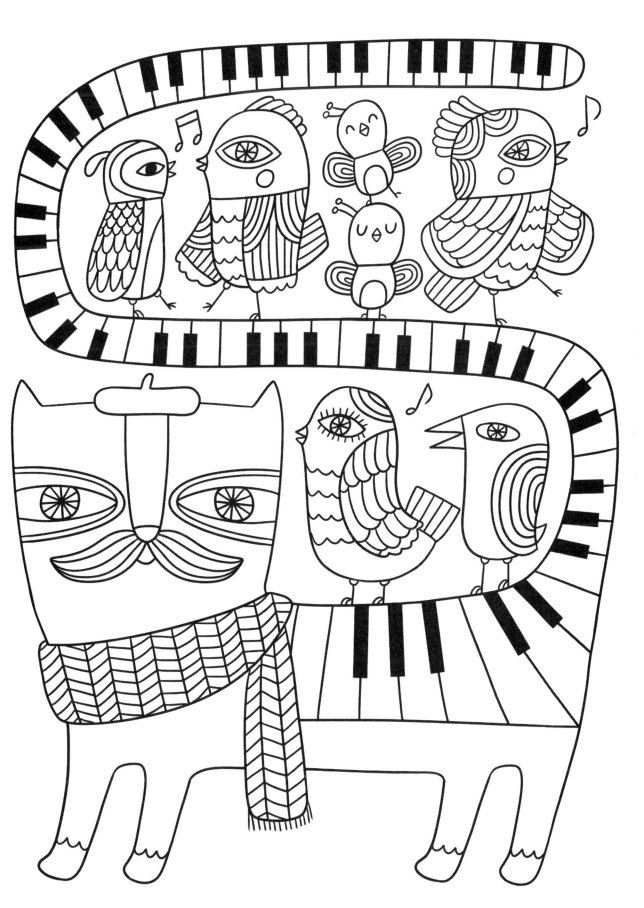

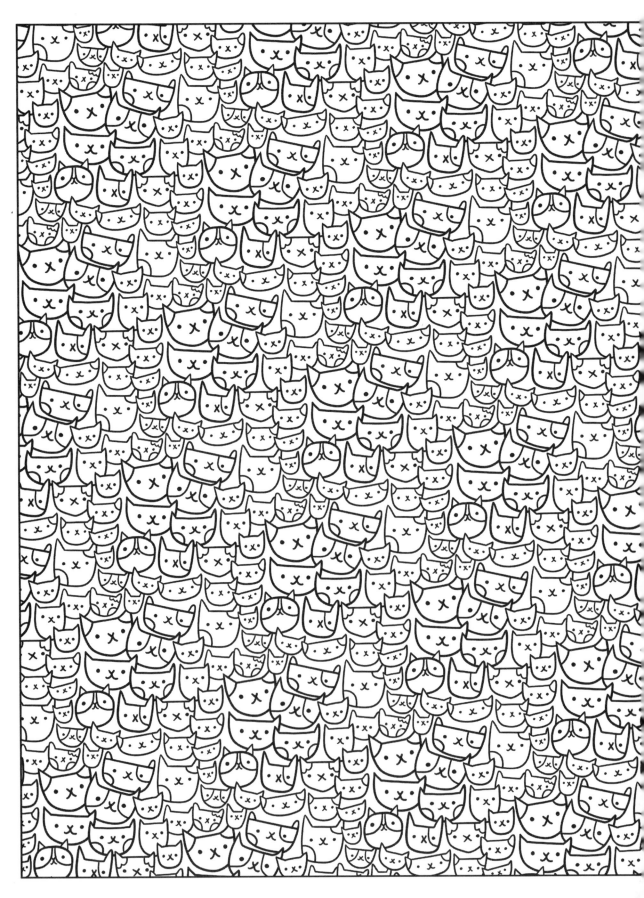

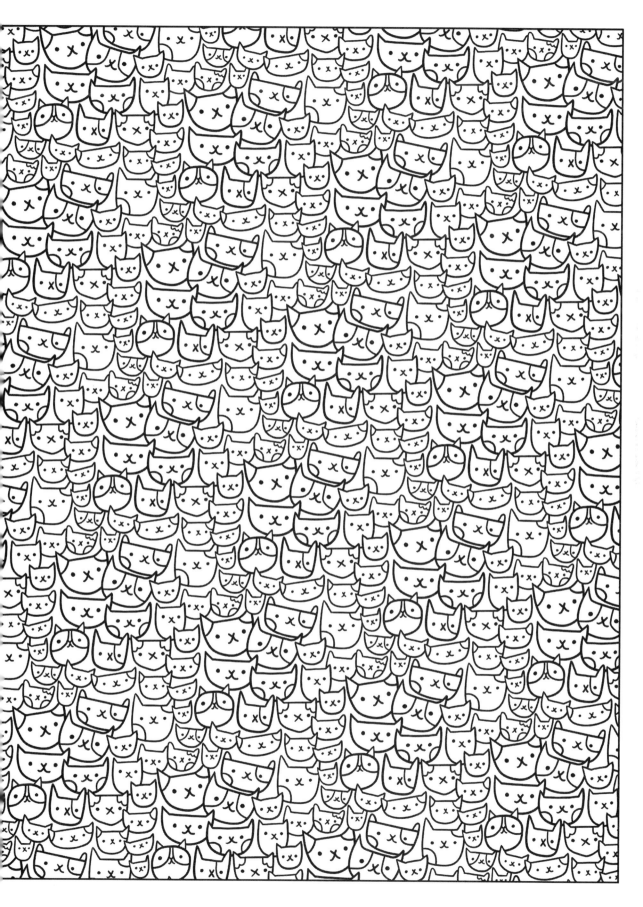

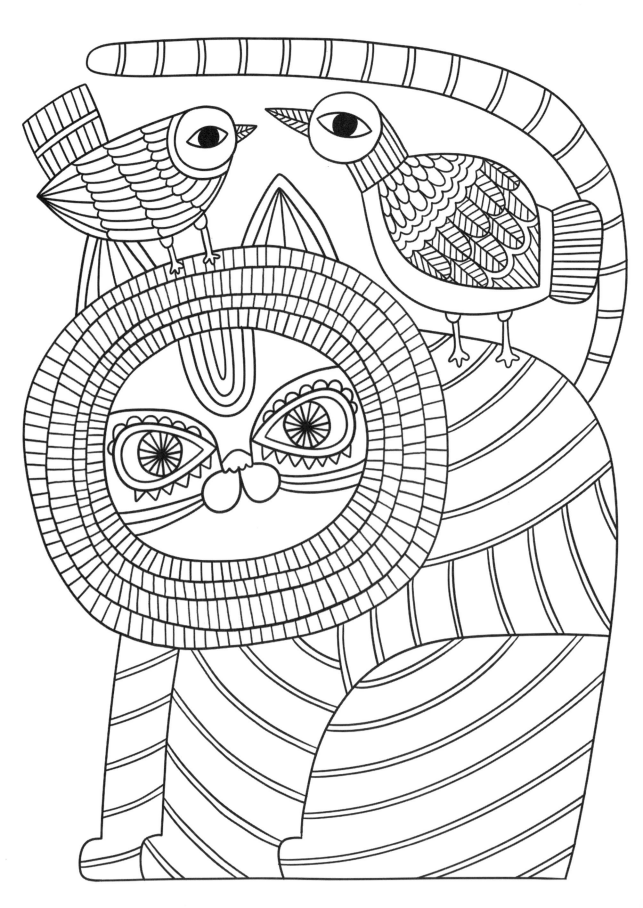

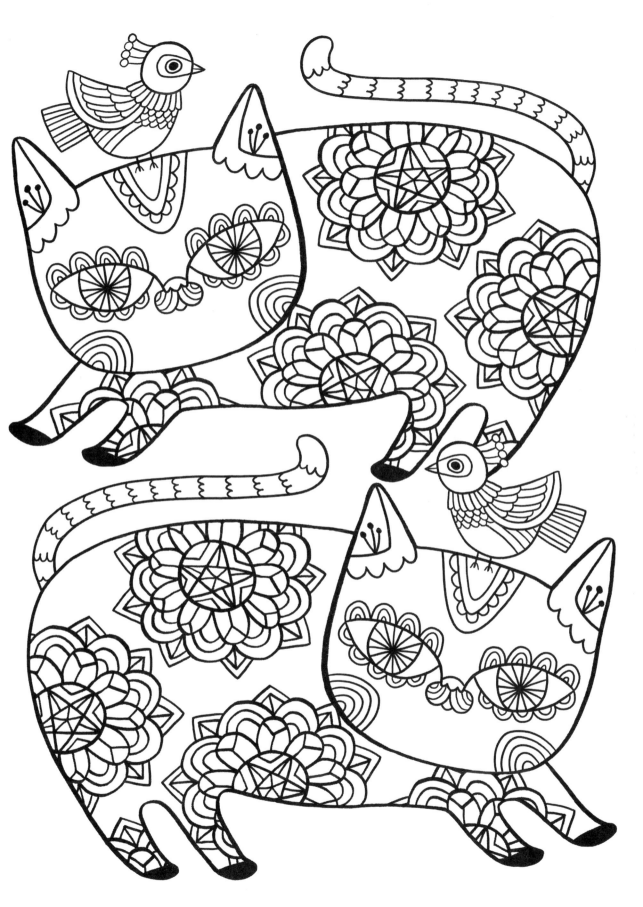

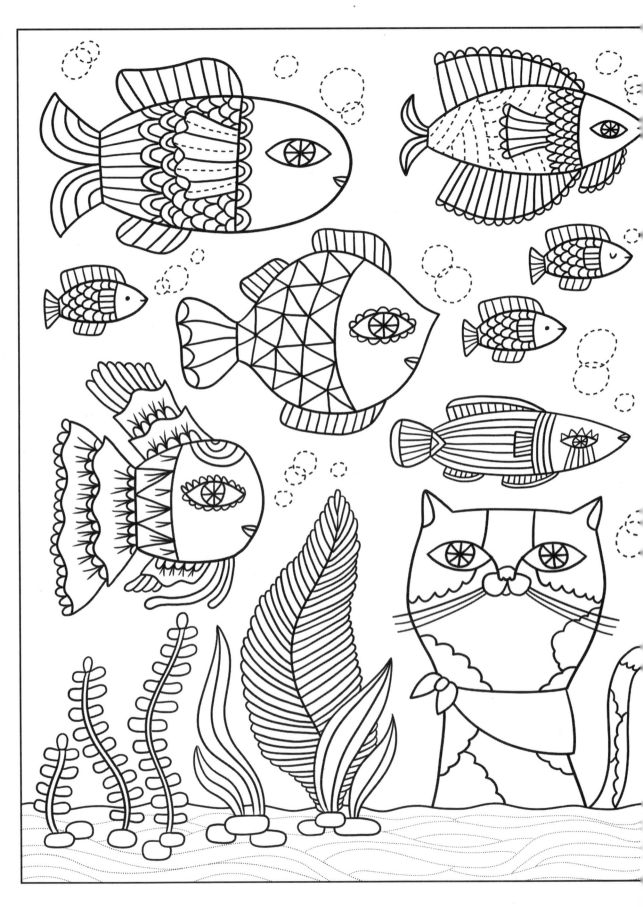

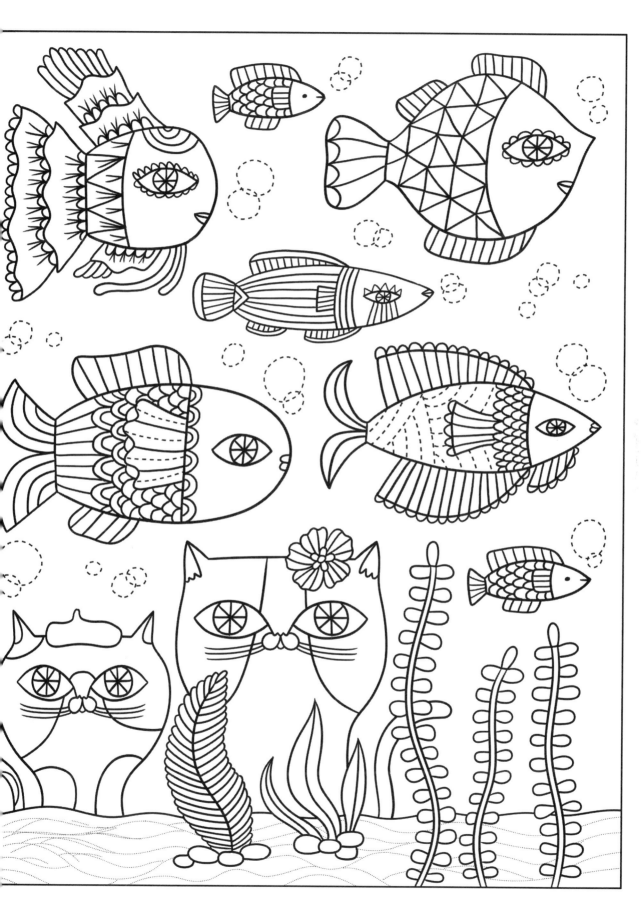

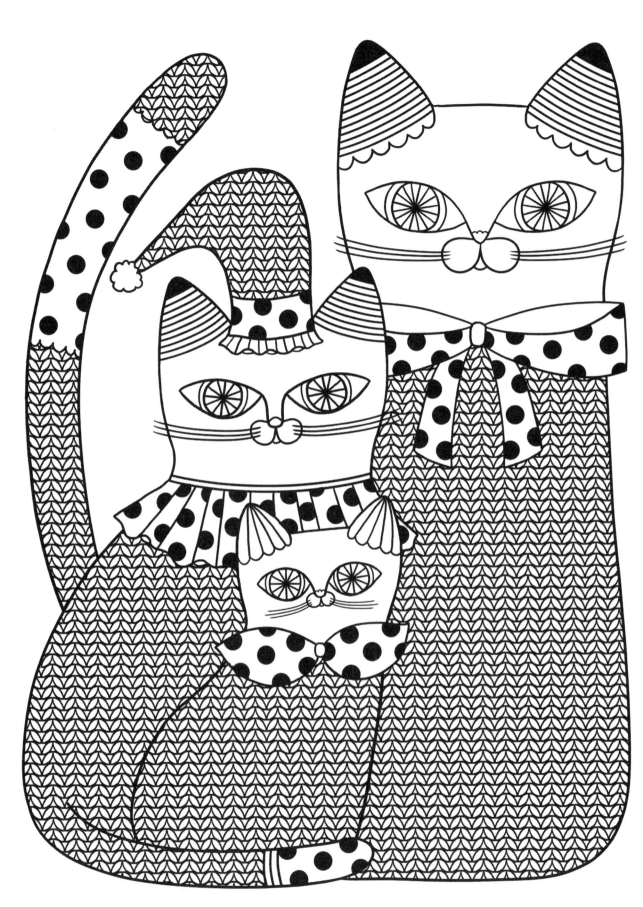

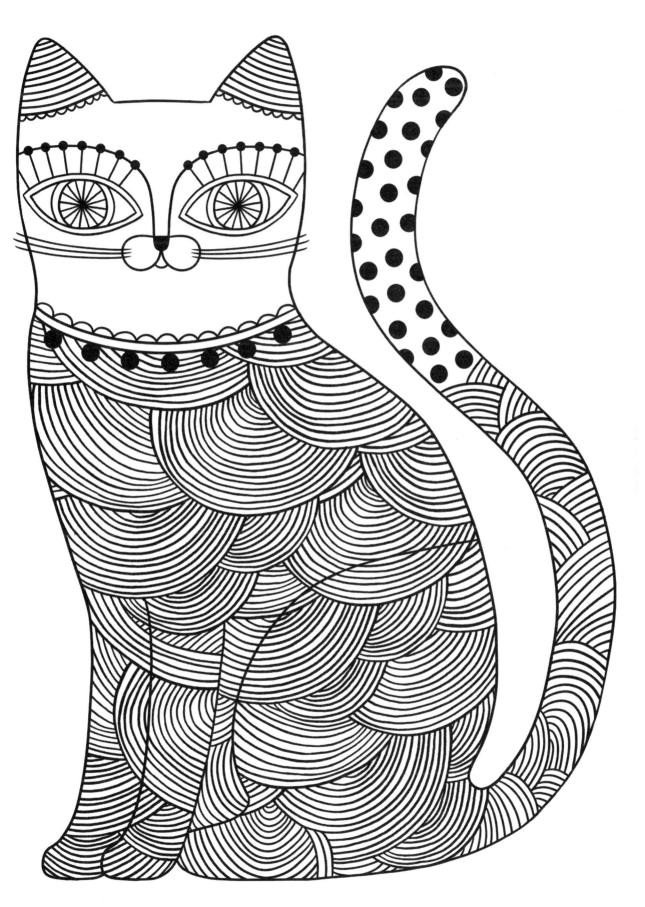

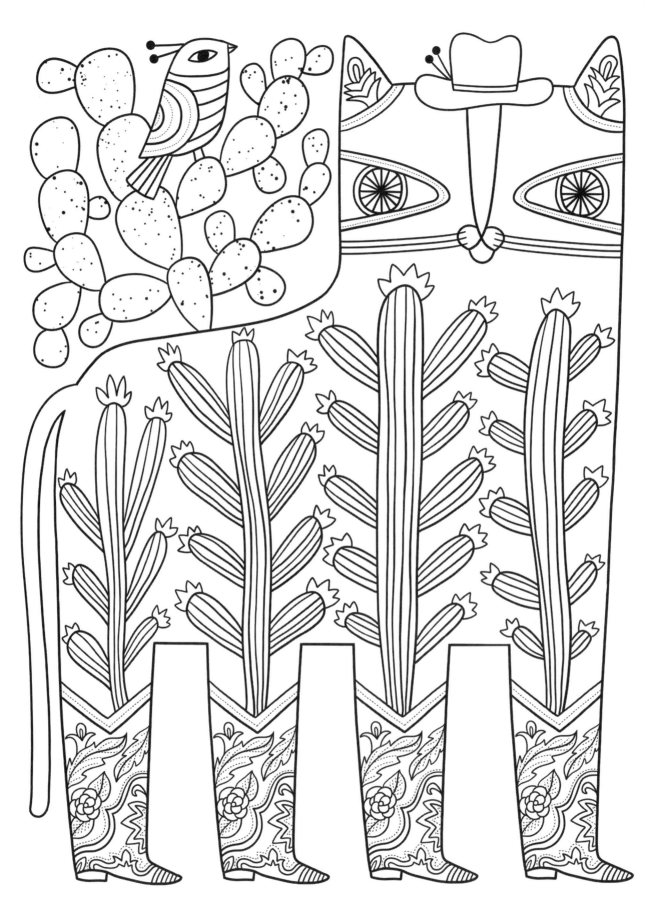

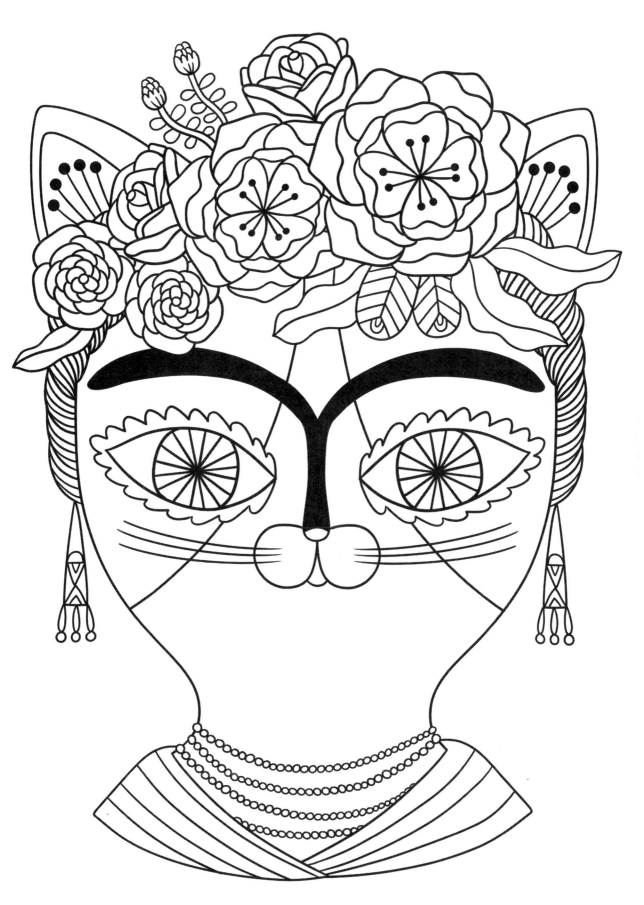

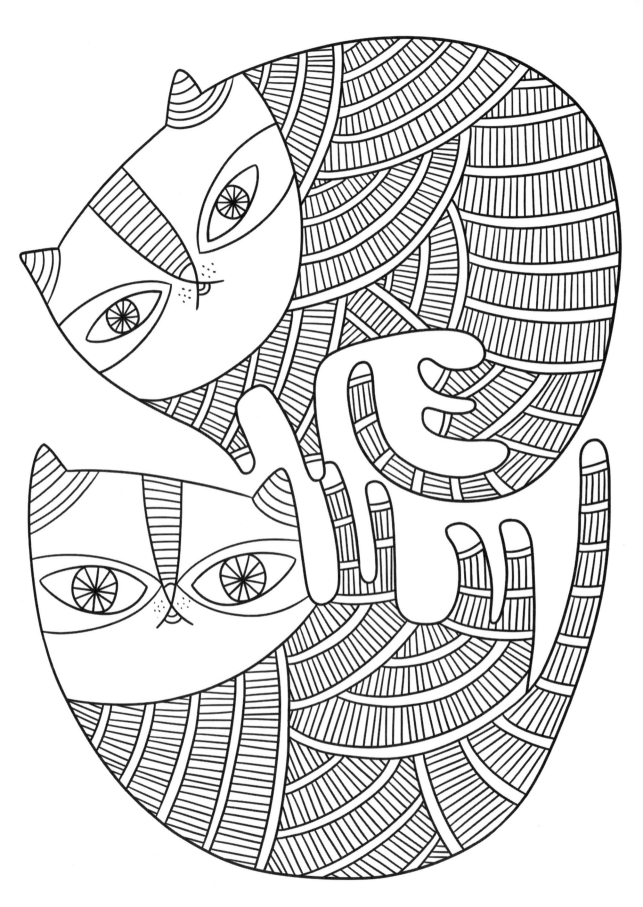

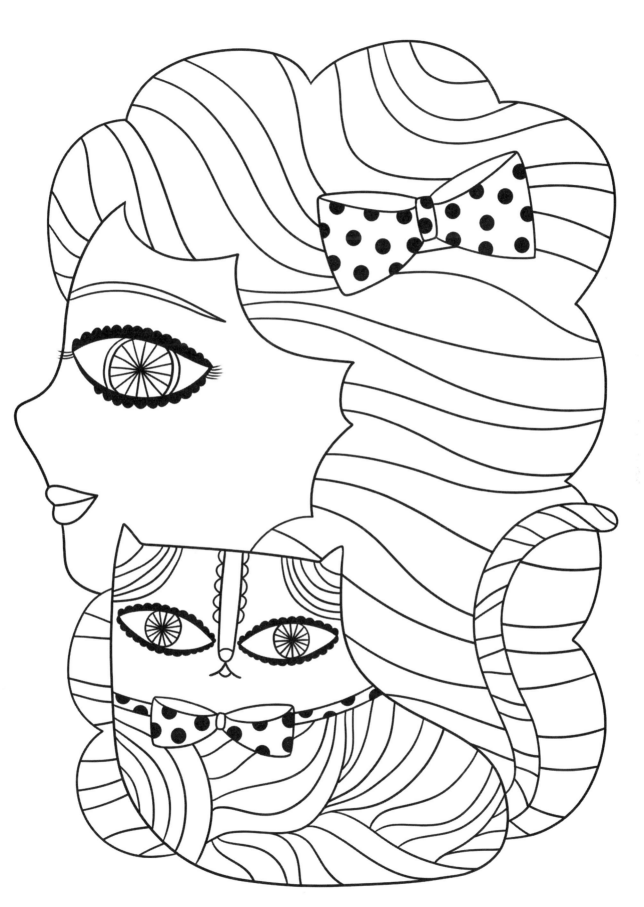

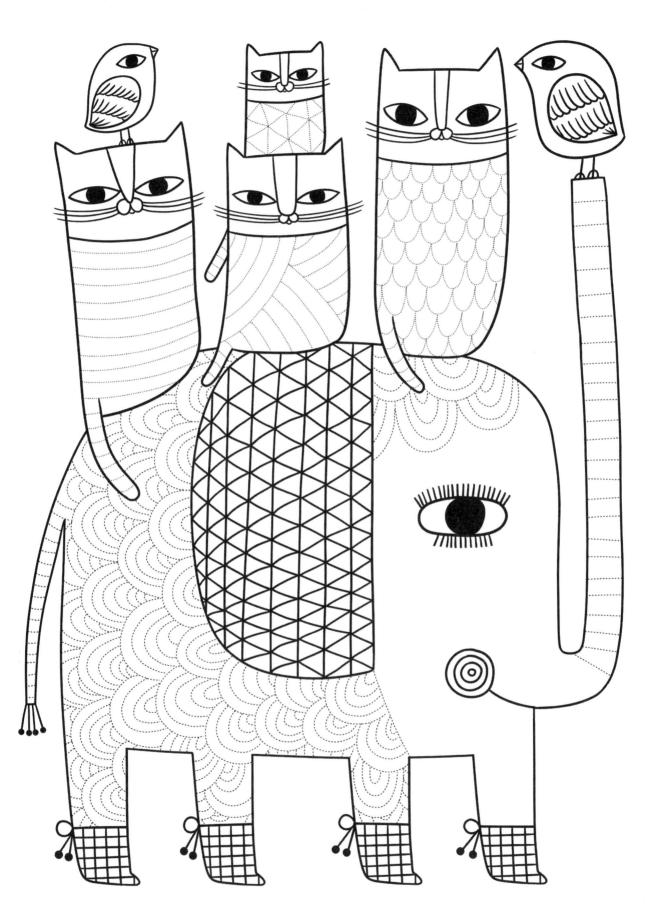

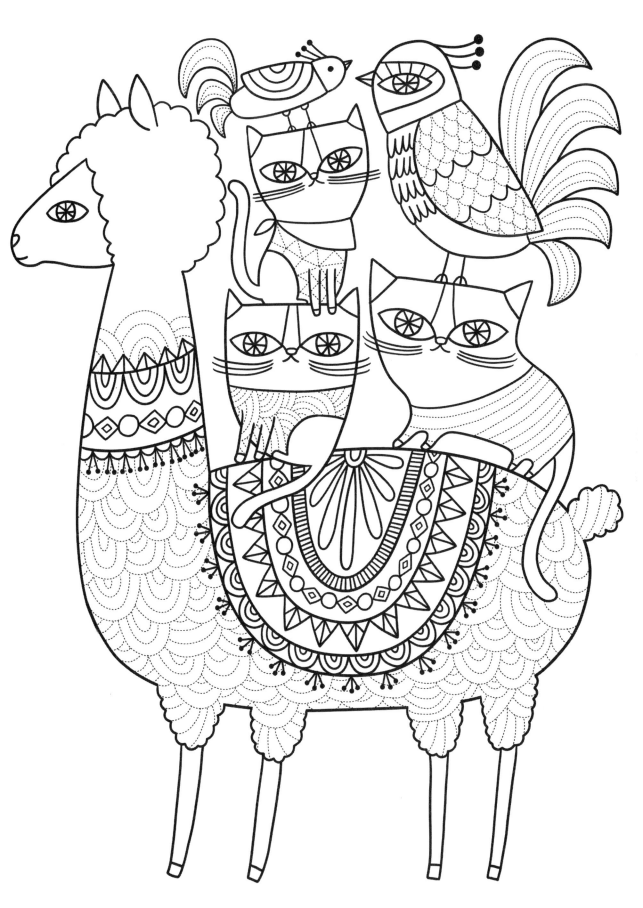

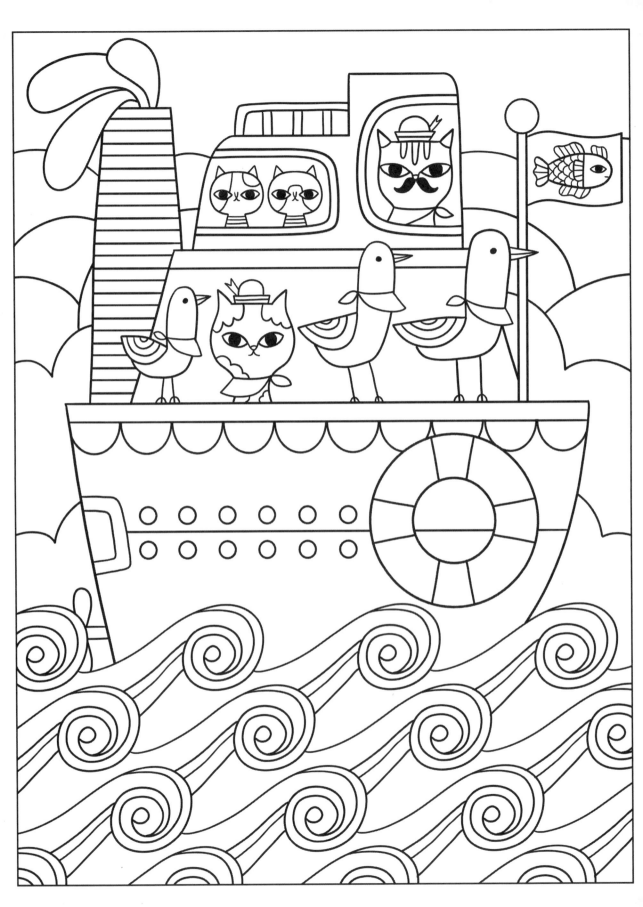

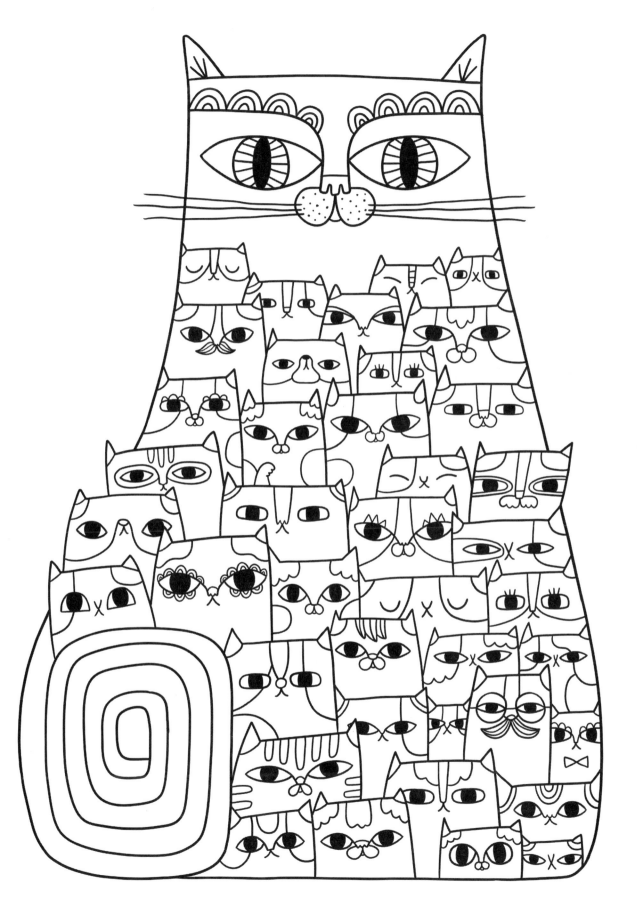

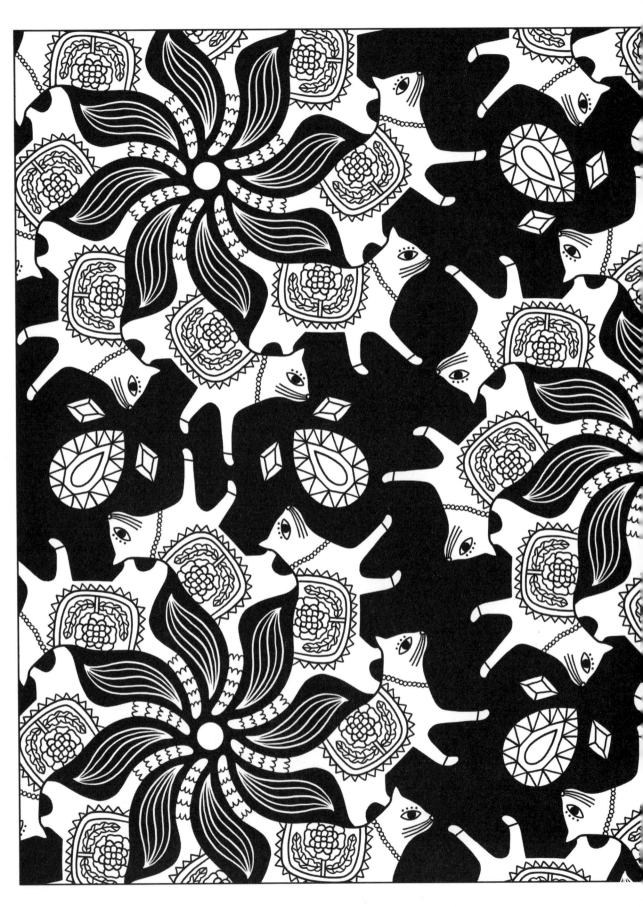

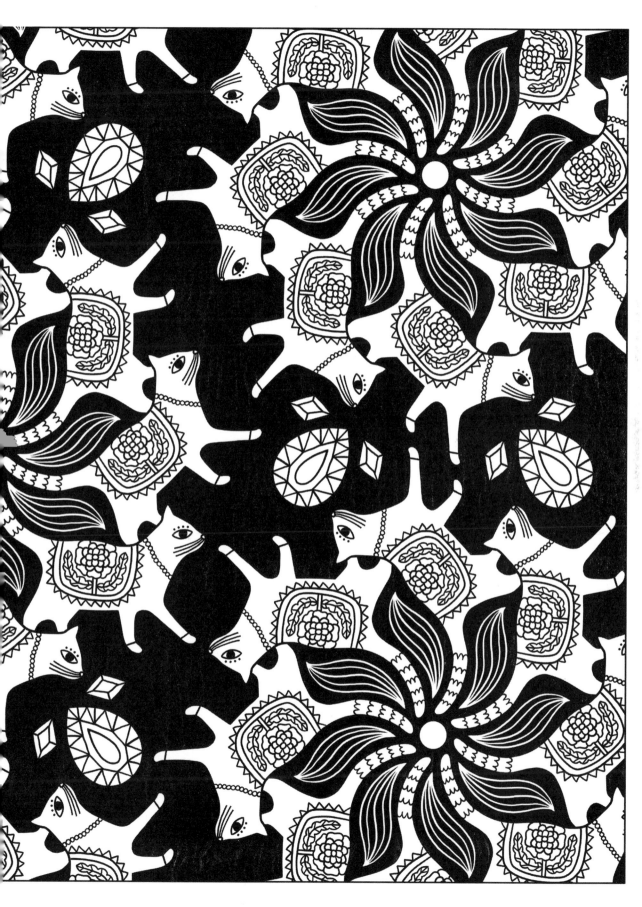

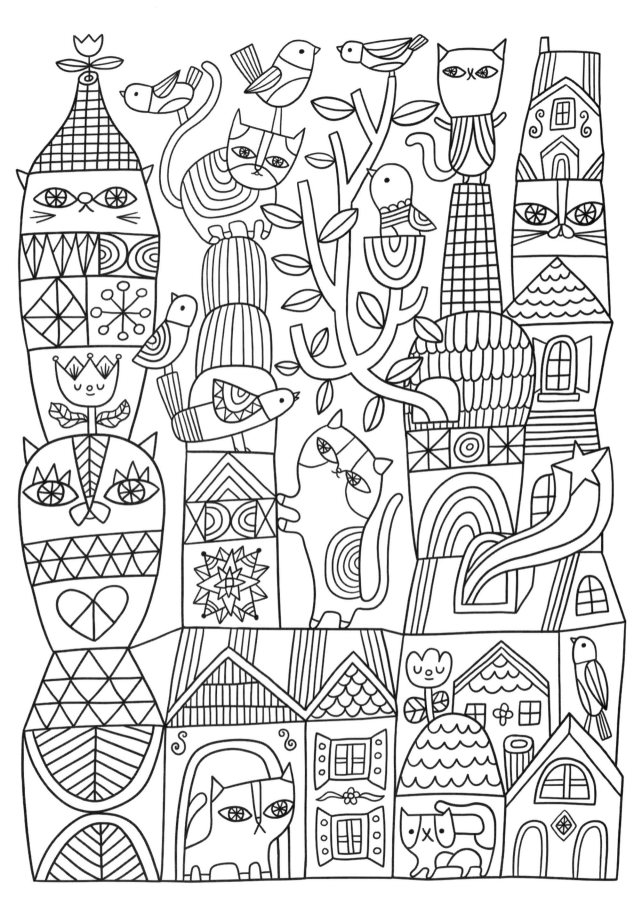

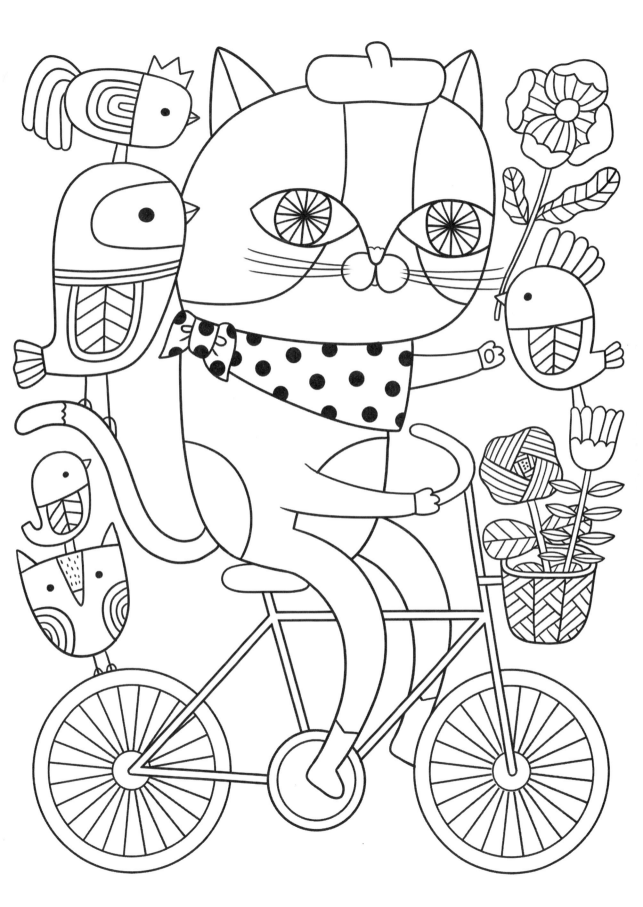

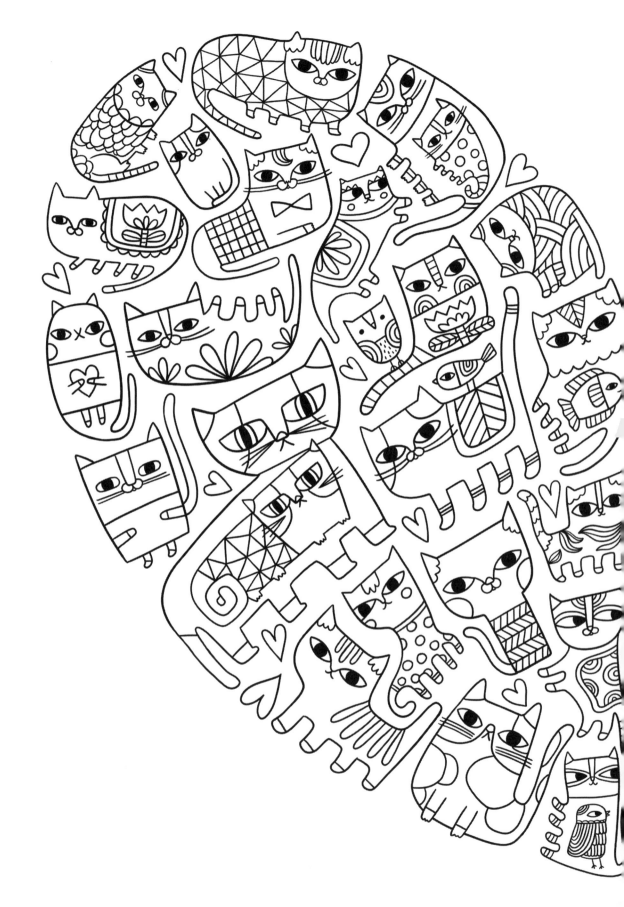

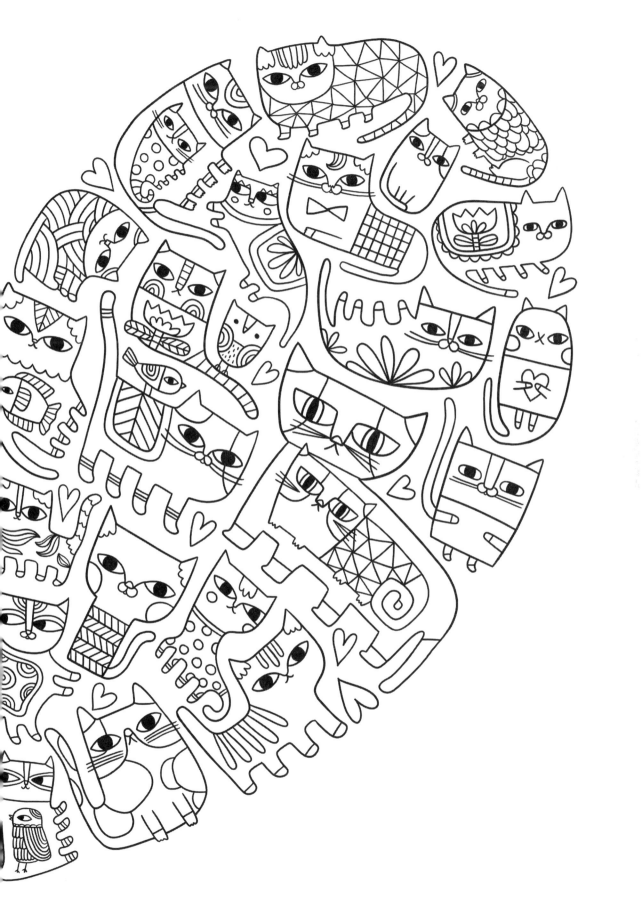

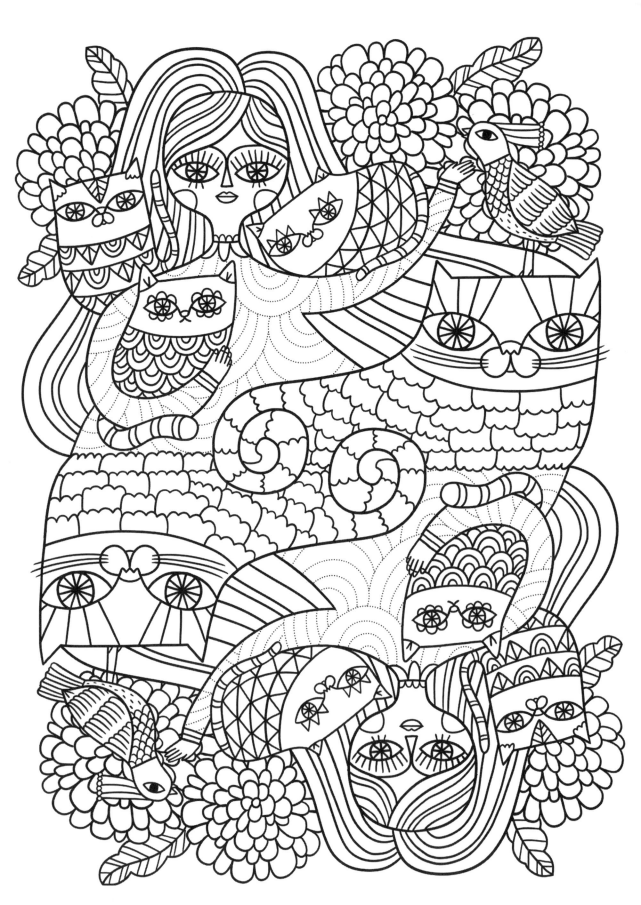

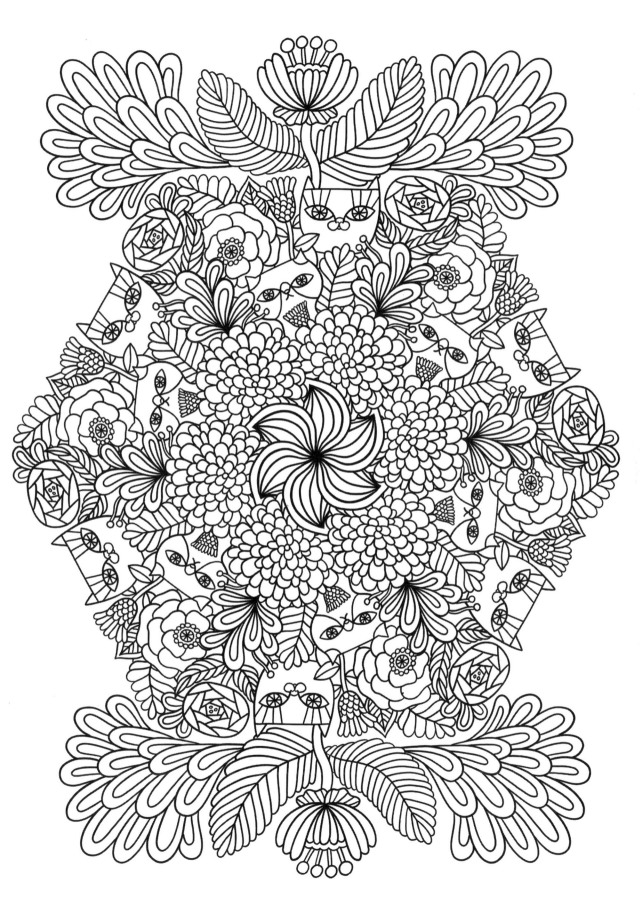

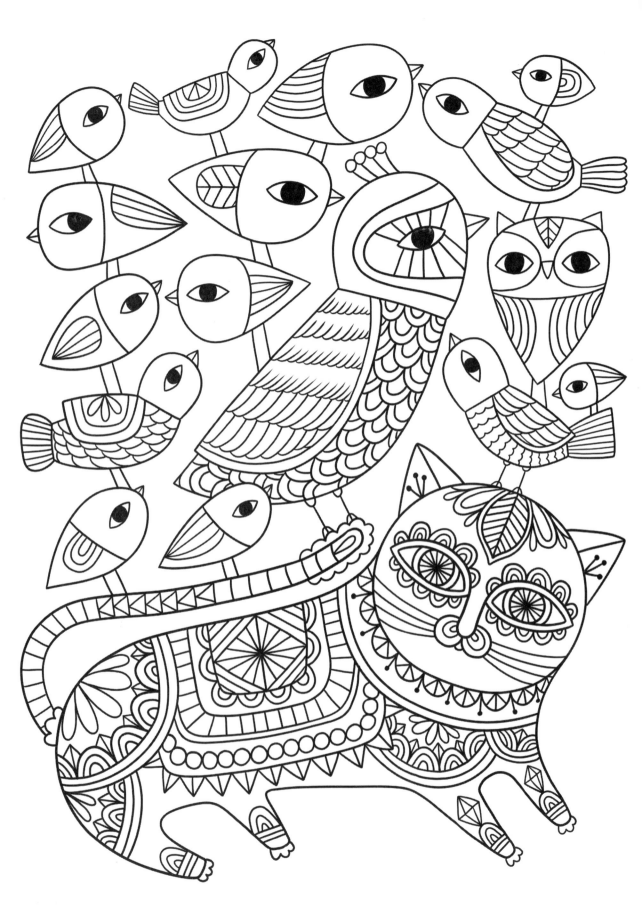

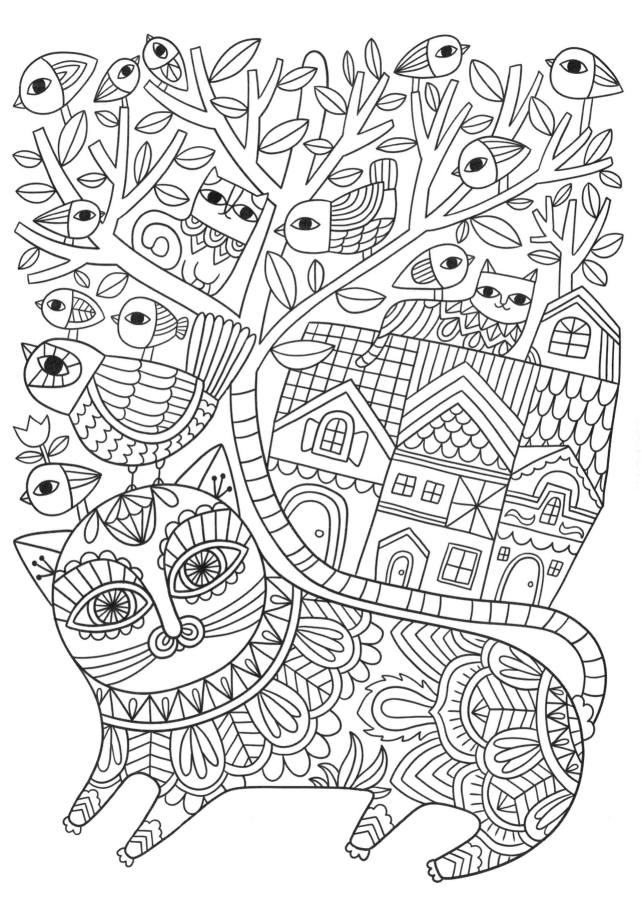

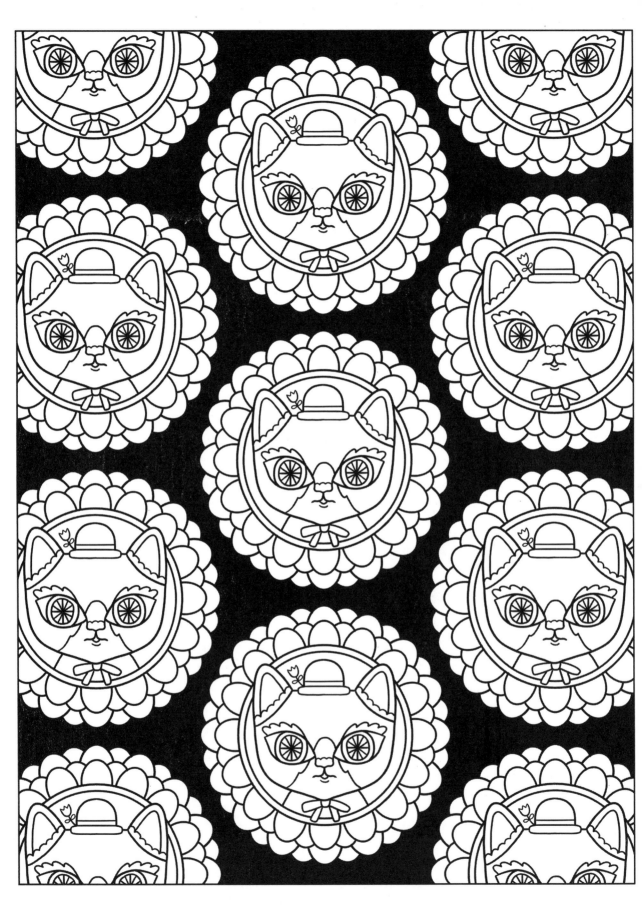

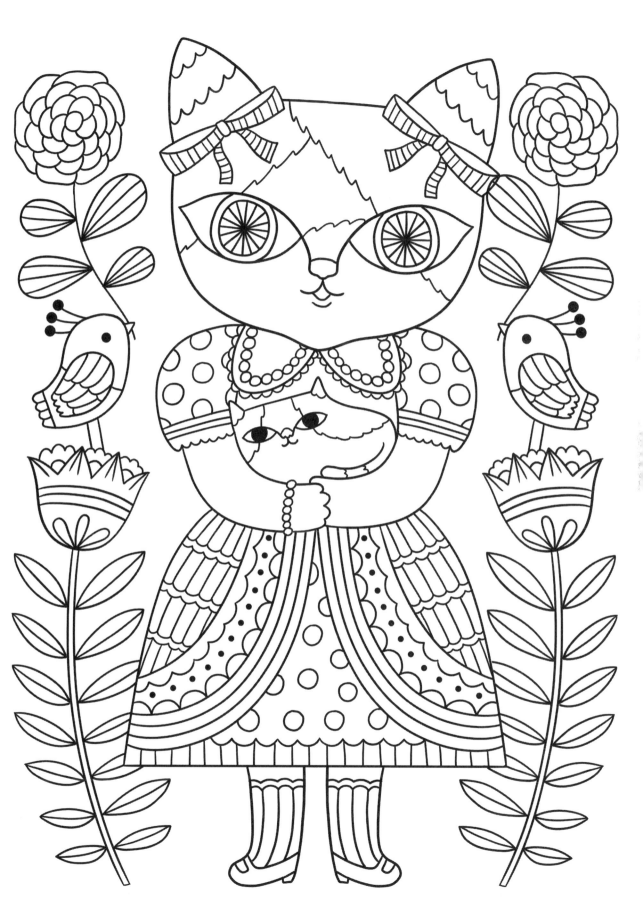

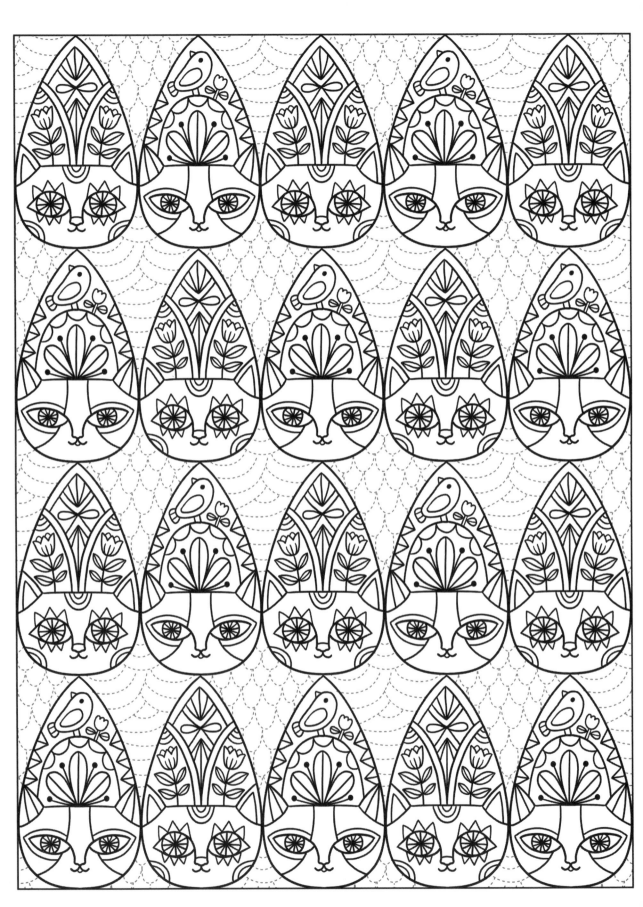

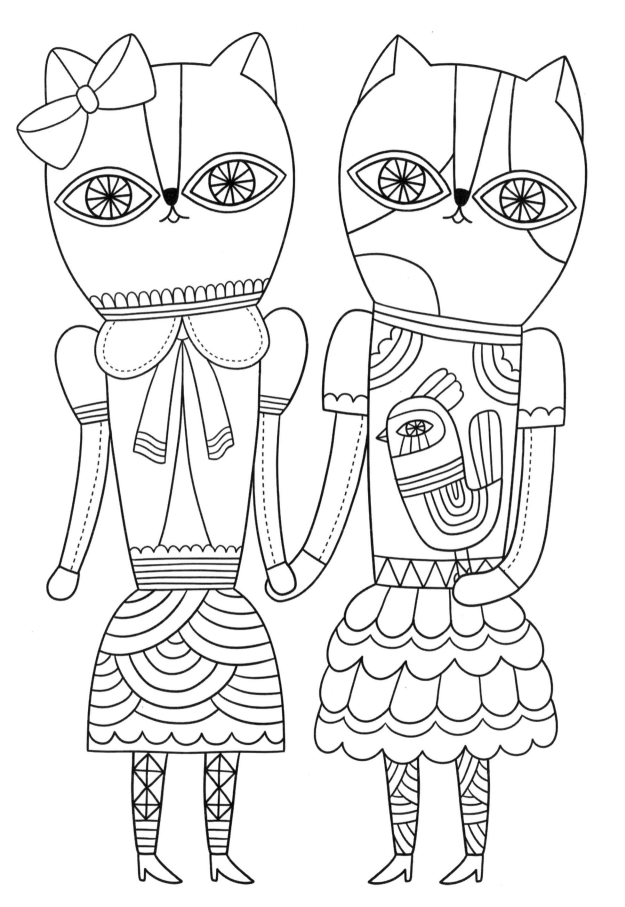

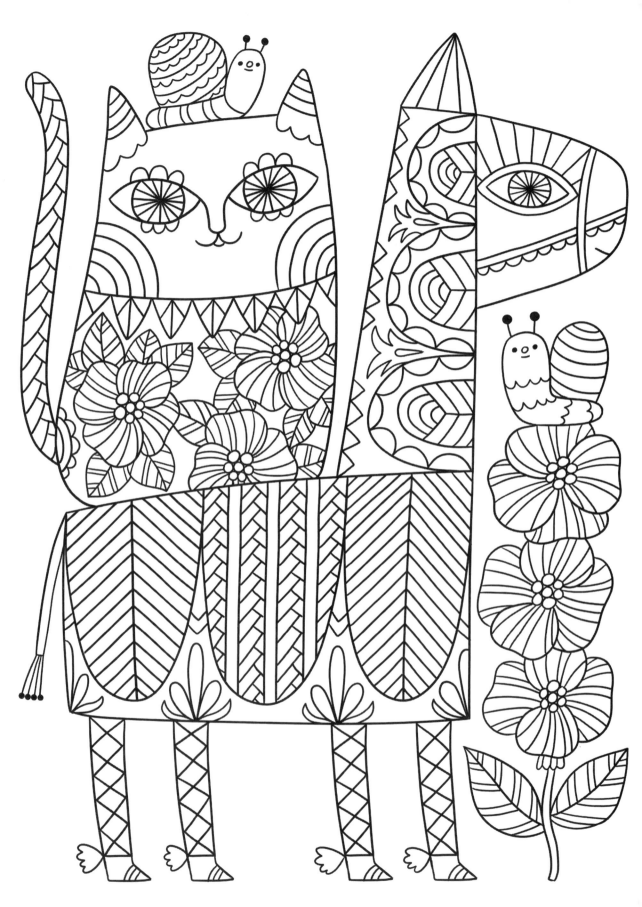

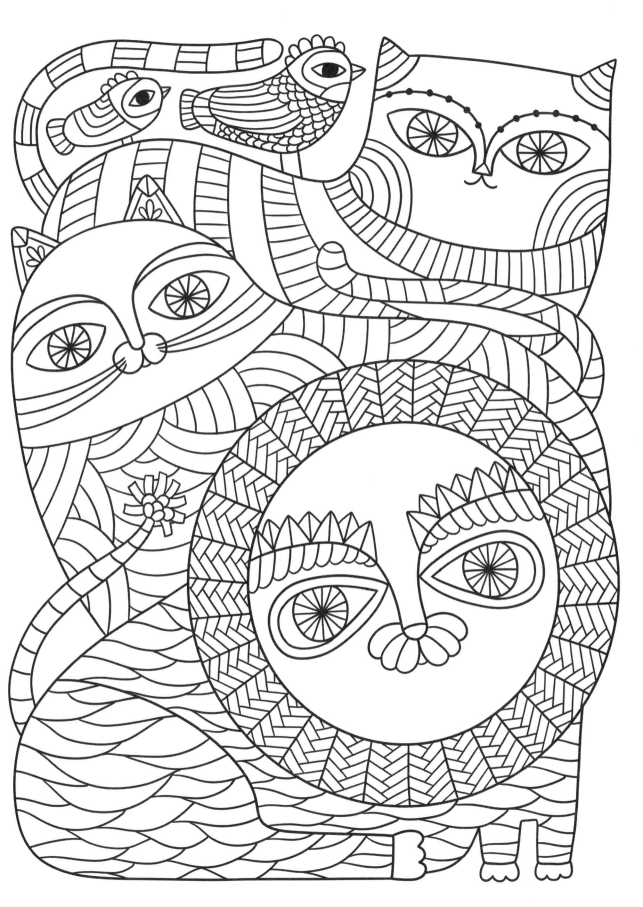

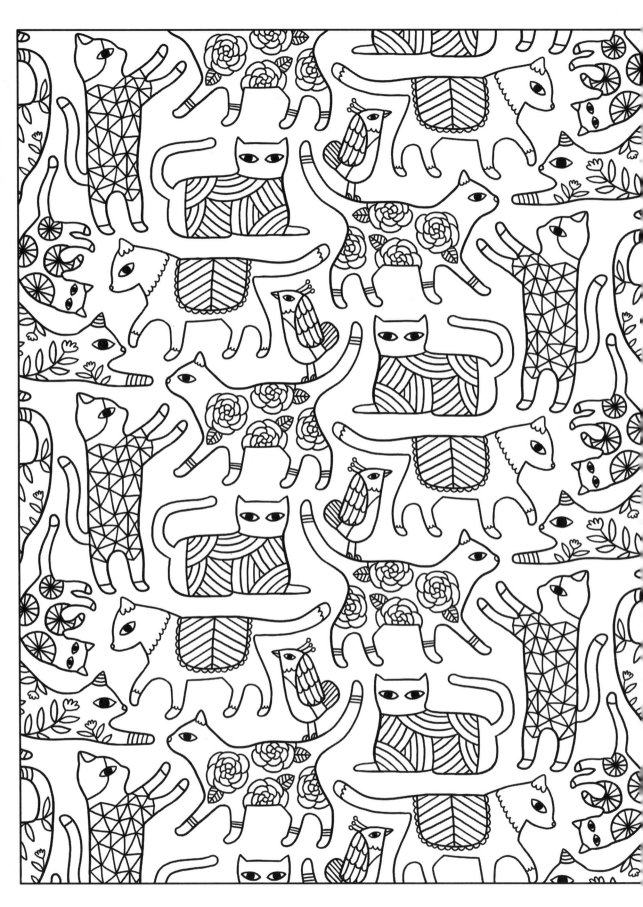